Juliana and Ranulf of Morpeth Castle

The earliest history of the Gospatric and de Merlay families

Bridget Gubbins
Cover illustration by Suzi Santorini

Published by
Greater Morpeth Development Trust
2016

By the same author

Newminster: Monks, Shepherds and Charters, 2014
The Mysteries of Morpeth's Workhouse, 2013
The Drovers are Coming to Morpeth Town, 2012
The Curious Yards and Alleyways of Morpeth, 2011
Published by Greater Morpeth Development Trust, with illustrations by Victor Ambrus

Power at Bay, 1977
Generating Pressure, 1991
Published by Earthright Publications

Published by
Greater Morpeth Development Trust
Carlisle Park Lodge
Castle Square
Morpeth
Northumberland
NE61 1YD

**Greater Morpeth
Development Trust**

© Bridget Gubbins   First published 2016

Cover illustration by Suzi Santorini
Back cover photo by Rosie Cusson

The two Bayeux Tapestry scenes, *Bishop Odo wielding his Club* and *Building a Motte* are Copyright Reading Museum (Reading Borough Council). All rights reserved.

The right of Bridget Gubbins to be identified as the author of this work has been asserted by her in accordance with the Copyrights, Designs and Patents Act 1988

British Library Cataloguing in Publication Data
A catalogue reference for this book is available from the British Library

ISBN   978-0-9568683-6-7

Cover design by Azure Printing

Printed in Great Britain by Martins the Printers Ltd., Sea View Works, Spittal, Berwick upon Tweed, TD15 1 RS

Acknowledgments

Greater Morpeth Development Trust, for their confidence and support
John Bibby, for reading and historical advice
Kim Bibby-Wilson, for reading and historical advice
Gail Boyes and Teresa Saunders, for Latin translation and guidance
Carol Colquhoun, for French translation
Rosie Cusson, for friendly travelling company in Normandy
Keith Elliot, for research guidance
Martine Gressant, mayor of Le Merlerault, for interest in historical links between our towns
John Griffiths, for reading and historical advice
Colin Pearson, for IT
Denis Peel, for photography
Frank Rescigno, for reading and art guidance

I would particularly like to express my gratitude to Ian Bower, librarian of the Society of Antiquaries of Newcastle upon Tyne, and all the staff at the library of the Literary and Philosophical Society for their endless help. We are fortunate that they guard their wonderful collections for the benefit of everyone.

People who helped in all kinds of other ways are credited in the text.

Unacknowledged photos and maps are by the author.

Hunting out the French connections in Normandy.
Above: Rosie en route
Left: Bridget with the mayor of Montbray and his helper

Contents

Acknowledgments
The couple at the castle
Key dates

*Map showing most significant places
mentioned in the text*

Juliana and Ranulph of Morpeth Castle

The earliest history of the Gospatric and de Merlay families

The couple at the castle

"Is this going to be the Romeo and Juliet story of Morpeth?" asked the director of the development trust.

I was discussing with him my idea to tell the story of the marriage of Juliana and Ranulph and its significance in the early years of the Norman Conquest.

Although I would have liked to do this, I had to say that it wasn't possible. We simply don't have any evidence of romance or tragedy. We have only a few bare historical records about either of them.

"Are you writing a story of Northumbrian women, and their courage and bravery, risking their lives every time they give birth, and suffering great indignities with forced marriages and the humiliation of widowhood?" my sister asked me.

I was thinking how I could bring to life the story of Juliana, the girl who came to Morpeth when she married the son of a Norman conqueror of England. We know little more about her than her name, but she had really existed, married and given birth to children, nine hundred years ago, in the town in which I live.

Had Juliana suffered great indignities? Certainly she would have risked her life giving birth, but there are no records about whether she endured humiliation of any kind. Her marriage was arranged, and the king had something to say about it. However, as that was the expectation for a daughter of the nobility in those days, perhaps she just accepted her role with its excitement and its uncertainties.

What about her husband, Ranulph, the son of the first baron of Morpeth, William de Merlay? He was a partner in this arrangement. His father and the king for political reasons favoured the alliance between the families of the conquering Normans and the exiled earls of Northumberland, the de Merlays and the Gospatrics. This marriage would help stabilise the borderlands between Scotland and England. The two young people were at the focus of this plan.

No, it could not be a Romeo and Juliet story. I had to think about what could realistically be told. Before I could even start, the big questions were – what do we know? Where are the sources? And how would I frame it?

My grandchildren gave me some ideas. They sometimes say: "Nana, tell us about when you were little and you were afraid of the horses!" or "Tell us the story of how Daddy threw the cake all over the kitchen!" Requests like these helped me understand that we hold about three generations of stories in our minds; our own, our parents' and our grandparents'. Further back than that, the stories become vague.

Of course we can study family history and learn more. Also, in days of yore, when long winter nights encouraged storytelling round the fireside, people's memories would have extended further back in time. Thus, I knew that Juliana would hold in her head the adventures of her grandfather who fought the Norman conquerors but ultimately lost the struggle, and her father and mother who grew up in exile in Scotland. She had her own story of her childhood and coming to Morpeth. In the same way, Ranulph would have heard time and again from his father about how he had left the family home in Normandy and taken part in the ferocious conquest of England.

Through these two young people, who didn't even speak the same language, I decided to investigate their stories, and to see what I could find out about Morpeth's earliest history. I would start with their grandparents and take it to the time of their marriage, over the course of three generations.

This is also a story about the countryside. We know virtually nothing about Morpeth in the days before and just after the Norman conquest of the north. Who was in charge? Who were the people who worked on the land? Was there even a village here? Juliana's grandfather lost the family's earldom in Northumberland, as we shall see. Was there any connection between his loss and Juliana's arrival in Morpeth?

A historical story needs to be told in an order. That means dates. In the case of long-distant and persons of minor national importance like Juliana and Ranulph, there are very few. I would of course use those, but I needed a more detailed structure, and I spent many an hour working on the possibilities - the dates for example of when Juliana and Ranulph married, and when their children were born.

In the end I worked out from a later date how previous events could have happened. If you look at the key dates table which follows, you will see near the bottom of the right hand column the date 1129, when Juliana and Ranulph's son William signed a charter. The historian Rev Hodgson has transcribed the charter, and you can see it on page 105 of his *History of Morpeth*. From this fact, and obviously as William was old enough to sign, it was possible to estimate that the couple had been married for 16 years or even longer. This single fact is fundamental to the story which follows.

As far as historical records show, William was the oldest of their children. The younger sons did not sign the charter. Perhaps they were too young to do so. In this case, William may have been about 15 years of age, and responsible enough to travel with his father and his aunt to Durham for the signing ceremony. The younger brothers would have stayed at home.

There may have been other reasons why the younger brothers did not sign, and that William was in fact older than 15. Those reasons would take Juliana's and Ranulph's marriage to an earlier date.

However, King Henry I had been involved in the marriage arrangements which were part of his plan to stabilise Northumberland in the years after he became king in 1100. Thus Juliana's and Ranulph's marriage must have taken place after 1100 and before 1129 when William was old enough to sign the charter.

Bearing these thoughts in mind, I placed the likely date of the marriage as about 1113. I was reassured as my investigations developed that few if any known dates clashed with this assessment. They all fitted into the basic framework. As we follow the stories, you can be aware, as I am, that the timing of the events is possible but never certain.

Like all historical stories of these remotely recorded times, the story is hedged with "possibly", "perhaps", "could have been", "it is likely", "it seems", and similar phrases.

What in fact do we know for sure? Juliana is mentioned by name in three sources; in her marriage charter, as a founder and donor to Newminster Abbey, and in her burial place with her husband and son Osbert at the abbey. These details are all recorded in an appendix to the Newminster Cartulary. We know more about the men of her family including her father and grandfather, but only the name of her mother.

As for Ranulph's father, William de Merlay, tracking down reliable sources of information about him is a story in itself as we shall see. We can learn a lot however from the way his life was linked to important historical characters, Bishop Geoffrey of Coutances who was one of William the Conqueror's most important men, and Robert de Mowbray, who became earl of Northumberland.

In the course of working on this story, a fascinating connection with a little town in Normandy called Le Merlerault has come to light. The place of origin of Ranulph's grandfather, Roger du Merle, in Normandy has not been known until this time. The story of that discovery is told at the beginning of Part 2.

Yes, I would really have liked to tell the story of the courage and bravery of a Northumbrian woman, Juliana. In the end, I settled for what she surely knew and held in her mind, and what she would have told her children. In the same way, Ranulph too would have heard his father's version of the conquest of England.

We start with Juliana's grandfather, Gospatric I, gleaning evidence from the chroniclers of his battles, changes of loyalty, victories, and ultimate defeat. In his rampagings, he crossed and re-crossed the north of England from his base in Bamburgh to his ultimate exile in Dunbar.

Ranulph's story takes us back to the preparation for the conquest of England, with his grandfather Roger's departure from the green fields of Normandy. His father William at that time was hardly more than a boy, and his career was closely linked with a warrior bishop and the future earl of Northumberland. These early chapters are gleaned from surviving historical documentation. They are based around men and their battles, and are very much from the perspective of the church chroniclers.

As the chapters progress, we move away from battlefields to the more homely elements, focussed on Morpeth. William de Merlay in Morpeth and Juliana's father in Dunbar are looking out for a suitable marriage for their offspring. Their ambitions will bring Juliana to Morpeth, not as a helpless girl but one who plays significant role.

Although we have so little evidence about Juliana's life in Morpeth, we can learn from other contemporary sources. As for the village people who worked in the fields around the castle and beside the Wansbeck, those whom she would see in her daily life, and whose language she spoke, we know virtually nothing about them. Nevertheless, we will work out what we can from what is available.

We will follow dramatic events and meet striking characters; Juliana's grandfather Gospatric who battled alongside the Danes against the Norman invaders; Geoffrey of Coutances, the warrior bishop; Ranulph's father William de Merlay who followed the bishop; the unpleasant Robert de Mowbray and the unfortunate Lady Matilda who married him.

These are exciting stories, and little told. Through them, we will learn how the Normans arrived in Morpeth as they gradually controlled Northumberland. We'll discover the first documented mention of Morpeth and the castle by the Wansbeck. So come along and explore with me the stories behind the marriage of Juliana, who came as young bride to Ranulph, the son of a conqueror, and the future baron of Morpeth.

Bridget Gubbins
Old Bakehouse Yard
Morpeth

Summer 2016

Gospatric key dates		de Merlay key dates	
		1030	Geoffrey of Coutances born
		1050	Roger du Merle and Emma Giroye married about this time
		1051	Wm de Merlay possible birth year
1060		1060	
		1066	**Battle of Hastings. Bishop Geoffrey of Coutances important participant** William de Merlay possible participant, possible age 15
1067	**Gospatric I, Juliana's grandfather, became earl of Northumberland**	1067	**Harrying of Yorkshire and Co Durham**
1070		1070	
1072	**Gospatric I deprived of earldom**		
1074	**Gospatric I died**		
1080		1080	**Bishop Odo's harrying of Northumbria**
		1085	**Robert de Mowbray became earl of Northumberland** circa 1085 William de Merlay obtained Morpeth barony circa 1085
		1087	**Death of King William the Conqueror** **King William II, Rufus, became king of England**
		1088	**Rebellion in south of England with Bishop Geoffrey and Earl Robert** **Trial of Bishop William de St Calais of Durham where William de Merlay addressed the king**
1090		1090	
		1091	**Bishop Geoffrey retired to Normandy. Died 1093**
		1092	William de Merlay and Menialda possible marriage year
		1093	**Earl Robert's men killed King Malcolm of Scotland**
		1093	Ranulph possible birth year
		1094	Goffrid possible birth year
		1095	Morel possible birth year
		1095	**Earl Robert's rebellion and capture** **First documentary mention of Morpeth castle**
		1096	Eustorcia de Merlay possible birth year
1098	Juliana possible birth year		
1100	**Henry I became king of England** Gospatric II given land in Northumberland after 1100	1100	**Henry I became king of England** **Between 1100 and 1129** **First Morwick charter of William de Merlay** Signed by his sons Ranulph, Goffrid, Morel
1110		1110	
1112	Juliana's marriage charter around this time		
1113	Juliana's marriage to Ranulph possible year, she aged 15	1113	Ranulph's and Juliana's possible marriage year
1114	Juliana's son William possible birth year	1114	William de Merlay possible birth year
		1115	Roger de Merlay possible birth year
		1116	Osbert de Merlay possible birth year
1120		1120	
		1129	**William de Merlay died** age 78 (if 15 at conquest)
1129	**Juliana and Ranulph's son William signed second Morwick charter,** possible age 15	1129	**Juliana and Ranulph's son William signed second Morwick charter,** possible age 15
1130		1130	
1138	**Juliana's father Gospatric II killed at Battle of Standard**	1138	**Foundation of Newminster Abbey by Ranulph de Merlay; donation of part of Juliana's dowry**

Dates in **bold print** are historically documented and fairly certain. Dates in normal font are possible, but there could be many alternatives. Ranulph and Juliana's marriage date is based on the 1129 signing of the Morwick charter by their son William, and Juliana's possible birth date is based on her possible age of 15 at the marriage.

PART 1   NORTHUMBRIANS   1066 - 1075

Gospatric I, Earl of Northumberland, Juliana's grandfather

Who was Juliana?

Juliana had grown up in exile from the family's ancestral lands in Northumberland. She was born probably in the late 1090s. Her grandfather Gospatric had been exiled by William the Conqueror, and given lands by the king of Scotland. We may guess that she lived with her parents and brothers and sisters at their castle at Dunbar, which is on a rocky outcrop by the sea. We can picture her playing among the waves with her brothers and sister, like any little girl. But she had a proud ancestry. It is certain that during the long winter evenings, as the family sat around the fire, the stories would have been told. She would learn about the adventures of the past, and as she grew older begin to wonder about her destiny.

The name Gospatric was used by three generations, her grandfather who we will call Gospatric I, her father Gospatric II, and her brother with whom she would have played by the sea, Gospatric III.

She was descended from the royal families of Scotland and England. Gospatric I's grandmother Bethoc was daughter of King Malcolm II of Scotland (1005 – 1034).

Gospatric I's grandmother Elfgiva, through his mother's line, was the daughter of King Ethelred II of England (978 – 1016).

Put another way, Juliana's great great great grandfather was King Malcolm II of Scotland. Juliana's other great great great grandfather was Ethelred II, king of England.[1]

Her grandfather was a cousin of King Malcolm III of Scotland (1058 – 1093).[2] Malcolm III married Margaret in 1069. Like Juliana, Queen Margaret was also a descendant of King Ethelred of England, who was her great grandfather. The kings and queens of Scotland played an important part in the lives of Juliana's family.

The men of the house of Gospatric were the warriors of their day. Galloping horsemen, with helmet and shield, and sword raised aloft; this was the the image they liked to portray of themselves - leaders who were proud, warlike and violent, the sort of men to follow into battle. We can see this on the seals to their charters.

---

[1] Rev Greenwell, The House of Gospatric, Northumberland County History, Vol VII, 1904, p 104
[2] There is some debate about whether or not they were cousins. See William Kapelle, The Norman Conquest of the North, London, 1979 p 108, who assumes he was; and Elsa Hamilton, Mighty Subjects, John Donald, 2010, p 8, notes, who puts the wider case. In this story, Malcom III and Gospatric I are taken as being cousins

The one on the left is from Juliana's brother, Gospatric III, who died in 1138. The one on the right is from a later descendant of the family, Patric I, earl of Dunbar, who died in 1231.[3] No seals survive from as far back as Juliana's grandfather Gospatric I, but he would surely have liked the same imagery. This was the world of the men in her life.

The name Gospatric comes from the British language which was spoken in Northumberland before the arrival of the Angles, or English. It derives from *Gwas Patric*, the servant of Patrick, probably referring to Saint Patrick. At the time, the name was not uncommon, so historians tell us, and Juliana's grandfather had perhaps been named after his uncle Gospatric who had been murdered in 1064.[4]

Gospatric I and the Norman conquest of the north
Everyone knows that Duke William of Normandy defeated the English in 1066 at the battle of Hastings, after which he became the king of England. Our story here is about Juliana's grandfather Gospatric and his part in the Norman conquest of the north. It explains why he acted as he did, how she ended up being born in exile, and provides the background to the story which brought her to Morpeth.

Juliana's ancestors saw themselves as descended from kings, and their base was the castle of Bamburgh. The great kingdom of Northumbria had once extended from the Humber to the Forth, and west to the Irish sea. But at the time immediately before the Norman invasion, it was a mere shadow of its former self.

The countryside here had been crossed and re-crossed, attacked and counter-attacked, ravaged and suffered, time after time. The Vikings had attacked Lindisfarne in 793, and returned in force in in 875 when they'd overwintered in the Tyne. In 934, King Athelstan of Wessex "went into Scotland with a land force and a sea force, and ravaged much of it". In 993, the Vikings attacked Bamburgh again.[5] King Malcolm II of Scotland attacked in 1006, and again in 1018 when he defeated the Northumbrians at the battle of Carham. Siward, earl of Northumbria, led an expedition north into Scotland against Macbeth in 1054.[6] Although there is no surviving evidence, many of these groups of warriors could have used the river crossing at Morpeth, ravaging the countryside as they passed.

As a result of all these disturbances, what remained of the northern part of Northumbria, the former kingdom of Bernicia, was weakened. It was threatened by the Scots from the north and the strong Viking kingdom in the south, based in York.

Danish Vikings, Scots, Northumbrians, English from the south had all rampaged through the countryside, attacking from the sea and penetrating the rivers. The dramas were far from over. Soon another set of invaders would be coming. They were also from far away, with yet another form of militarism, and a different language.

As she sat on her father's knee in their castle in Dunbar, Juliana would hear the stories about her grandfather's adventures first hand. We however must glean what we can from chroniclers who told the stories not long after the events.

One was Simeon of Durham. Among the works associated with his name were *History of the Kings* and *History of the Church of Durham* in the early eleventh century.

The other was Orderic Vitalis, a monk of the monastery at Evroult in Normandy. He had been sent there from England as a child. He wrote *The Ecclesiastical History of England and Normandy*.

---

[3] Rev Greenwell, pp 37, 44 and 55
[4] As above, p 16
[5] Anglo Saxon Chronicles, Anne Savage, Bramley, 1997, p 144;
[6] Kapelle, The Norman Conquest of the North, London, 1979,p 46

The new king of England, William the Conqueror, had many rebellions to deal with in the south, and he needed a strong earl to control the north. In 1067 he appointed Copsig, a Dane from York, but he was killed by Northumbrians when they set fire to the church in which he was hiding at Newburn on the Tyne. Soon after that, Juliana's grandfather Gospatric I enters our story.

He approached the foreign king in December 1067, and offered him a sum of money. William accepted it, and agreed that he should be the authorised earl of Northumbria.

> At Osulf's death, Cospatric, the son of Maldred, going to king William, obtained the earldom of the Northumbrians, which he purchased for a great sum; for the dignity of that earldom belonged to him by his mother's blood.[7]

By accepting him, William gained money that he needed. At the same time, having Gospatric on his side could be an advantage in controlling an unruly part of his new kingdom. But he took a risk. Gospatric was a cousin of Malcolm III, king of Scotland, who had his own reasons for thinking Northumberland should be part of his kingdom.

Taxes for the north? No thank you   1068
The situation was chaotic. King Swein of Denmark had his own claim to the throne of England, and was threatening. Edgar Atheling, grandson of the former king Ethelred, thus related to the earls of Bamburgh, also had a claim to the throne. Malcolm III of Scotland, Gospatric's cousin, was planning to invade.[8]

Because King William needed money to maintain his army, he levied great taxes between December 1067 and March 1068. The new earl Gospatric and other northerners wouldn't accept this. They joined a rebellion and headed for York, crossing the rivers of Northumberland, ready for battle.

Orderic described these events.

> All joined in a determined league and bold conspiracy against the Normans for the recovery of their ancient liberties. The rebellion broke out with great violence in the provinces north of the Humber. The insurgents fortified themselves in the woods and marshes, on the estuaries and in some cities. York was in a state of the highest excitement, which the holiness of its bishop was unable to calm. Numbers lived in tents, disdaining to dwell in houses lest they should become enervated; from which some of them were called savages by the Normans.[9]

---

[7] Simeon, History of the Kings of England, (from now on, abbreviated to Simeon, Kings), Llanerch, 1987, p 139 and 144
[8] Kapelle, pp109-110
[9] Orderic Vitalis ,Ecclesiastical History of England and Normandy, Thomas Forester, London, 1854, Vol 2, Bk II, p 18

King William led his army north, having his troops quickly erect timber castles as part of his battle strategy. The same type of castle would be erected by the Norman conquerors beside the Wansbeck a little later. Orderic recorded this new kind of warfare.

> In the English districts there were very few fortresses, which the Normans call castles; so that, though the English were warlike and brave, they were little able to make a determined resistance.[10]

The northerners retreated from their tents, and slipped away. Gospatric found refuge with King Malcolm III in Scotland. Allied as he was to Edgar Atheling, he was part of the party which included the future queen Margaret of Scotland. This account of the story is from Simeon.

> Marleswen and Gospatric, and some nobles of the Northumbrian race – to avoid the severity of the king, and dreading that like others they might be put in confinement, taking with them Eadgar Atheling and his mother Agatha, with his two sisters Margaret and Christina – went by sea to Scotland, and there, by the favour of Malcolm, king of Scots, they passed the winter.

> King William went with his army to Nottingham, where he fortified the castle, and then marched to York, where he fortified two castles, and placed in them five hundred soldiers.[11]

The Northumbrians and the other rebels had not been subdued. Some, like Gospatric, sheltered in Scotland. Others were waiting in readiness at home.

Slaughter at York

William had to decide how to proceed. He appointed a Norman, Robert de Comines, as bishop in Durham, but the Northumbrians wouldn't accept him either.

> In the third year of his reign, king William sent earl Robert surnamed Cumin, to the Northumbrians on the north side of the Tyne.[12] But they all united in one feeling not to submit to a foreign lord, and determined either that they would put him to death, or that they all would fall together by the edge of the sword.

> The Northumbrians, marching all night with haste to Durham, at dawn burst the gates with great force, and slew on every side the earl's men, who were taken unawares … They then proceeded to attack the bishop's dwelling in which the earl had been received; but not being able to withstand the javelins of the defenders, they burnt the house with its inhabitants … almost all parts of the city were flowing with blood; for of seven hundred men none but one escaped.[13]

The Anglo Saxon chronicle records that 900 men were killed with Comines.[14] Feeling confident because Durham was crushed, Gospatric and the rebels moved south from Scotland towards York. Orderic tells the story.

> Marlesweyn, Cospatric, Edgar Atheling, Archill… with other powerful and fractious nobles, collected their forces, and joining a band of townsmen and their neighbours, made a desperate attack on the royal fortress of York.

> The king flew to the spot, and fell on the besiegers, none of whom he spared. Many of them were taken prisoners, numbers slain, the rest put to flight. The king spent eight days in the city, making an additional fortification.[15]

The Anglo Saxon chronicle records that "the Atheling went again to Scotland"[16]. At the same time, a stronger, wilder force was approaching to tackle the French-speaking conquerors, and Gospatric and his allies were getting ready.

---

[10] Orderic, Vol 2, Bk II, p 19
[11] Simeon, Kings, p 135
[12] This is presumably an error
[13] Simeon, Kings p 136
[14] Anglo Saxon Chronicle, English Historical Documents, p 149; Savage, p 199
[15] Orderic, Vol 2, Bk VI, p 22
[16] Anglo Saxon Chronicle, English Historical Documents, p 150; Savage, p 149

Dragon ships and Northumbrian warriors

In September 1069, two hundred and forty dragon ships were sailing towards the Humber. The Danes in their longboats were coming.

Gospatric and his followers, horsemen and men on foot, crossed the rivers and fields of Northumberland and headed south towards York. Their own fleet of ships was sailing to join up with the Danes. Despite having become King William's man only a year earlier, Gospatric then preferred to ally with a future Danish king rather than a Norman.

> Harold and Cnut, sons of Suane, king of the Danes, and their uncle earl Osbern, and their bishop, Christian, and earl Turkill, coming with two hundred and forty ships from Denmark, landed at the mouth of the river Humber. There they were met by Eadgar Atheling, earl Walthev, and Marlesswein, and many others with a fleet which they had provided. Earl Cospatric was there also, with the whole strength of the Northumbrians, who all assembled with one consent against the Normans.[17]

The Danes arrived on Thursday 8 September. They moved up the Humber, allowing time for Gospatric and other rebels to join them.[18] On Saturday 19 September the Normans in charge of York, realising the threat, set fire to the wooden houses there in case they might "be of use to the Danes in filling up the moats", as Simeon put it.

> For before the whole city was burnt, the Danish fleet arrived on the Monday, and the Danes assailing the castles on one side, the Northumbrians on the other, they took them by storm the same day. And more than three thousand of the Normans being slaughtered ... the Danes returned to their ships with untold spoils, and the Northumbrians to their abodes.[19]

Gospatric and his Northumbrian men slipped away, doubtless with their share of the "untold spoils". Some probably went by sea, and others by land, and once again the country people along the way would suffer as a hungry army passed through. The victors would boast about their successes as they went along. Three thousand of the Norman invaders had been killed at York. Wise old heads would shake in fear. There would be consequences.

When he heard the news, King William was furious. He would take his revenge.

The harrying of the north   1069

The king had been involved in battles in Wales, but he marched his army north. When he reached York, he found the city deserted.

King William set his men to work in what became known as *the harrying of the north.* His soldiers burned and slaughtered. The year 1069 was long-remembered, long-mourned, in the north.

> So great a famine prevailed that men, compelled by hunger, devoured human flesh, that of horses, dogs and cats. Others sold themselves to perpetual slavery, so that they might in any way preserve their wretched existence; others, while about to go into exile from their country, fell down in the middle of their journey and gave up the ghost. It was horrific to behold human corpses decaying in the houses, the streets, and the roads, swarming with worms, while they were consuming in corruption with an abominable stench ... Meanwhile the land being thus deprived of any one to cultivate it for nine years, an extensive solitude prevailed all around.[20]

King William decided to celebrate Christmas 1069 in York, and sent to Winchester for his royal regalia. He ate and drank amid the misery of the hapless population, as Orderic told us.

---

[17] Simeon, Kings p 136
[18] Kapelle, p 114
[19] Simeon, Kings pp 136-137
[20] Simeon, Kings p 137

While the war was in progress, William ordered the crown and the other ensigns of royalty, and plate of value, to be brought from Winchester, and stationing his army in camps, went himself to York where he spent the feast of Christmas.[21]

"Woe to thee Gospatric"

While the harrying of the north was going on, Gospatric had been taking advantage of the disruption. Bishop Agelwin of Durham decided that he and his monks should flee with the valuable body of Saint Cuthbert, and Gospatric had had his eye on the riches of the church. He advised the bishop to flee, according to these reports by Simeon.

> While the king was doing such deeds as these around and near York, Agelwin bishop of Durham, and the chiefs of the people, fearing lest ... the king's sword should include equally the innocent and the guilty in indiscriminate slaughter, with one consent betook themselves to flight, carrying with them the uncorrupted body of the holy father Cuthbert.[22]

> It was owing chiefly to the advice of this Cospatric that the fugitives had abandoned the church; and it was he who carried off with him the larger proportion of its ornaments.[23]

The bishop and the monks fled from Durham with the relics of their saint, who seemed to be watching over them and who performed a miracle.

> They made their first stay at Jarrow, their second at Bedlington, the third at Tughall, and the fourth at Holy Island. But about evening, when the full tide would prevent travellers from crossing over, behold by its sudden recess it left the approach clear for them ... but when they reached the land, lo! the sea coming up covered the whole sands as before.[24]

Earnanus was one of the monks who arrived with the precious relics on Holy Island. Later, he was sent back to Durham for news, and while sleeping in the course of the journey he had a vision which prophesied woe to Gospatric. He was in front of the altar in Durham, where Bishop Cuthbert and Saint Oswald were standing.

> The bishop [Cuthbert], indignant it seemed, at the desertion of the church, said, "Woe to thee, Cospatric! woe to thee, Cospatric, thou hast pillaged our church of its possessions, and hast turned it into a solitude.[25]

In his dream, Earnanus accompanied the two saints to the edge of the city of Durham here he saw a deep valley filled with the souls of men. One of Gospatric's servants, Michael, was in hell.

> Therein this Gillo Michael was being tormented with fearful torments; for he was stretched at length in a filthy spot, and was suffering intolerable agonies, being pierced through and through with a sharp hay scythe. The wretch was screaming out, and sending forth, without intermission, fearful yells, dire howls, and pitiful groans.

> When I [Earnanus] recounted his intolerable agonies to earl Cospatric, and had added thereto what I had heard the saint say about himself, he trembled with fear, and immediately proceeded barefoot to the island where that holy body was; and by prayers and gifts he sought forgiveness for his transgressions. Yet this notwithstanding, he never afterwards recovered the honourable position which he had formerly enjoyed; for having been expelled from the earldom, the remainder of his life was a series of misfortunes and adversity.[26]

Somehow, the story of the proud Gospatric humbly crossing the sands barefoot doesn't seem true to character. We will see later if the prophecy of Saint Cuthbert came true.

---

[21] Orderic, Vol 2, Bk IV, p 29
[22] Simeon, Kings, p 137
[23] Simeon, History of the Church of Durham, (from now on abbreviated to Simeon, Church), p 688
[24] Simeon, Kings, p 137
[25] Simeon, Church, p 688
[26] Simeon, Church, p 688-690

Treasure and bounty to Bamburgh castle   1070

Also taking advantage of the disturbances in England, King Malcolm lll of Scotland raided Cumberland, and then headed east into Northumbria.[27] This is Simeon's account.

> During the same time, a countless multitude of Scots marched through Cumberland under the command of King Malcolm, and turning to the east ravaged with fierce devastation the whole of Teesdale and the parts bordering it on each side.

> … thence savagely overrunning the territory of St Cuthbert … he destroyed by fire the church of St Peter, the prince of the Apostles, at Wearmouth. He burned also other churches, with those who had taken refuge in them. While he was riding along the banks of the river, feasting his mind and eyes with such a spectacle, it was told him that Edgar Atheling and his sisters, who were beautiful girls of the royal blood, lay with their ships in that harbour. When they came to him, he addressed them graciously, and he pledged himself to grant them and all their friends a residence in his kingdom as long as they chose.[28]

As ever looking out for his own advantage, Gospatric and his followers turned and plundered Cumberland, which his cousin Malcolm considered his own.

> Amidst these pillagings and depredations of the Scots, earl Gospatric having called in some bold auxiliaries, made a furious plundering attack upon Cumberland. Having done this with slaughter and conflagration, he returned with great spoil, and shut himself up, with his allies, into the strong fortress of Bamborough, from which making frequent sallies, he weakened the forces of the enemy; for Cumberland was at that time under the dominion of king Malcolm, not by right, but subjugated by force.

> Having heard (while still gazing on the church of St Peter as it was being consumed by the fire of his men) of what Gospatric had committed against his people, Malcolm, scarcely able to contain himself for fury, ordered his troops no longer to spare any of the English nation, but either to smite all to the earth or to carry them off captives under the yoke of perpetual slavery.

> Some aged men and women were beheaded with the sword; others thrust through with pikes, like swine destined for food; infants snatched from their mother's breasts were thrown high into the air, and in their fall were received on the points of lances … Young men also and maidens, and whoever seemed fit for toil and labour, were bound and driven before the face of their enemies, to be reduced in perpetual exile to slaves and bondmaids … Scotland was, therefore, filled with slaves and handmaids of the English race; so that even to this day, I do not say no little village, but even no cottage, can be found without one of them.[29]

This is a clear if dramatic description of the consequences of these raidings for the ordinary folk of the countryside. Although Gospatric's family in Bamburgh was not on the losing side, they might well have been thankful that in this case at least it was not they who were sent into slavery.

As the booty arrrived at the fortress, Gospatric's wife, his mother and the women of his family would be obliged to feed and entertain the warriors. The booty would be piled up, counted, and divided among Gospatric's followers. There would be drinking, feasting and noisy celebrations, doubtless with boasting and tales of valorous deeds. Yet the more thoughtful among the family would surely have felt a confusing sense of split loyalties as they in their time had received hospitality from king Malcolm. Although this time, they were the victors, there was always the fear of retribution from the terrifying foreign conqueror.

The continuing intensity of king William's harrying of the north finally caused Gospatric to decide that he had better submit to the king.

> The indefatigable king pursued his desperate foes to the river Tees, through such difficult roads that he was obliged sometimes to dismount and march on foot. He remained seven days on the Tees. There he received the submission of Waltheof in person, and of Cospatric by his envoys

---

[27] John Beeler, Warfare in England, Cornell University, 1966, p 47
[28] Simeon, Kings, pp 138-139
[29] Simeon, Kings, p 139

who swore fealty on his part. Their former allies, the Danes were now exposed to great perils, having become wandering pirates, tossed by the winds and waves.[30]

Northumberland north of the Tyne was spared from the harrying, this time at least. After accepting Gospatric's submission, the king allowed him to continue as earl. Gospatric had been sufficiently humiliated. The arrangement would change in the future perhaps, but for the time being they were both making compromises.

Gospatric's downfall   1074

For a short time the king still seemed to need Gospatric, and asked him to escort the new Norman bishop Walcher from York to Durham.[31]

Then, in 1072, King William decided to do something about King Malcolm III's attacks on the north of England. He headed north, both along a land route which crossed the rivers of Northumberland, and by sea.

> King William set out for Scotland with a force both of sailors and men-at-arms, to reduce it to subjection … but when the king of the English had entered Scotland, king Malcolm met him at the place called Abernethy, and became his homager. William returning thence deprived Cospatric of the dignity of his earldom, charging him with having afforded counsel and aim to those who had murdered the earl Robert de Comines and his men at Durham, although he had not been present in person; and that he had been on the side of the enemy when the Normans were slain at York.[32]

Thus was Gospatric I humiliated. He was no longer needed to protect Northumberland from the Scots. He and his family were forced into exile. Despite their recent enmity, once again, King Malcolm came to his aid.

> Flying therefore to Malcolm, he not long after made a voyage to Flanders; returning after a little time to Scotland, the aforesaid king bestowed upon him Dunbar, with the lands adjacent in Lothian, that out of these he might provide for himself and his family until more prosperous times should come.[33]

The ancient earldom of Northumberland no longer belonged to his family. He'd fought rapaciously, changed allegiance several times, and greedily amassed booty. In the end, exile was the fate of his family.

Until more prosperous times should come

Dramatic as it must have been, there may have been an understanding that this situation was not permanent. Simeon wrote "until more prosperous times should come". Gospatric's lands in Northumberland lay between the areas controlled by King Malcolm and King William, neither of whom could be sure of his loyalty. The two kings may have come to an arrangement. The modern historian Elsa Hamilton suggests the following.

> Clearly, he could become a thorn in the flesh of both kings. Should we envisage therefore a further conversation at Abernethy in which both Malcolm and William recognised that at least one of their problems could be solved by removing this dangerous, unpredictable, charismatic earl from Bamburgh to Dunbar? … We might even speculate that Gospatric was a party to the Abernethy agreement, a participant in the arrangements for his future and for the future of the Northumbrian earldom.[34]

We know that Gospatric's granddaughter Juliana returned to Northumberland. As we follow her story, we will see if she would become part of the more prosperous times in the future.

---

[30] Orderic, Vol 2, Bk IV, p 29. For a splendid description of the Danish invasion and the king's retaliation, see pp 24 - 30
[31] Simeon, Kings, p 142
[32] Simeon, Kings, p 142
[33] Simeon, Kings, p 144
[34] Hamilton, pp 21-23

Saint Cuthbert's prediction of woe

Gospatric had a woeful end, as St Cuthbert had prophesied to Earnanus. By 1074, he was ill. His wild and eventful life was nearly over.

The story of his death was written by the 12th century chronicler Roger Hoveden.

> But after a short time had passed, Gospatric being in extreme ill-health summoned to him the monks Ealdwine and Turgot, who were at that time living for Christ's sake in poverty of goods and spirit at Melrose. And after a thorough confession of sins, and many lamentations of penitence, he ended his life at Ubbanford, which is Norham, and was buried in the exit of the church.[35]

A different version relates that he became a monk in Durham and died there. The stone lid of a coffin was discovered in 1821 during an excavation of the monks' cemetery. Engraved on it was the name *Cospatricus Comus*, Cospatric the count.

> It may be that the cover belongs to the coffin of the first Gospatric, the warrior of royal and aristocratic blood who for decades had fought and plundered and schemed and struggled; and who suddenly believing that he was facing death, turned his back on the world and sought peace and salvation as a monk in the convent of Durham where his bones still lie.[36]

Here we will leave this great Northumbrian warrior who had battled among the borderlands between Scotland and England. He had sons and daughters who would carry on his family's story from their place of exile in Scotland. But his life had run its course, and ended in the church beside the Tweed, or perhaps in the quiet of the convent in Durham.

It is time now to look at the Norman side of our story. While Juliana's grandfather Gospatric I was fighting here in the north of England, the tale of her future husband Ranulph begins with his father's participation in the conquest of England. It starts far away. There are some mysteries to be solved, and a journey which takes us over the sea to Normandy.

---

[35] Alan Orr Anderson, translator, Early Sources of Scottish History, Paul Watkins, Stamford, 1990. Translated from Chronicles of Roger de Hoveden, Vol 1, p 59, ed Wm Stubbs, London 1868
[36] Hamilton, pp 30-31

Le Merlerault and Morpeth

My sister and I were cycling in Normandy in the summer of 2014. We had a few scraps of information in our heads about the places of origin of some of the players in the family story of Ranulph de Merlay, Juliana's future husband.

The historian of Northumberland, the Rev John Hodgson, informed us that Ranulph's father, William de Merlay, had served as a *serjeant* to Geoffrey de Mowbray, Bishop of Coutances about the time of the Conquest.[37] We could go to Coutances.

Percy Hedley, in his book *Northumberland Families,* had told us that Montbray was the home village of Bishop Geoffrey and his nephew Robert who later became the earl of Northumberland. We could go there too.

All that information was fairly secure. But with the de Merlay family, it was different. "It is not known from which part of Normandy or France the de Merlays took their name," wrote Percy Hedley.[38]

My sister and I enjoyed visiting Coutances where the later impressive gothic cathedral had replaced the original one built by Bishop Geoffrey around the time of the conquest of England. We cycled through country lanes to the tiny village of Montbray where the mayor and his *adjoint* kindly showed us the fields where once the *motte* of the de Mowbray family had been.

They took us inside one of the village churches where there were two huge 19th century oil paintings of their famous bishop. One was of him at the foundation of his cathedral. The other was of his deathbed scene. The caption to this second one listed all those present, and among them was the Bishop of Durham. We felt quite a sense of shock. Here in this little place among the green fields of Normandy was a link with the north east of England.

This was very interesting and satisfying, but what we really wanted was the place of origin of the de Merlays.

We consulted a road atlas looking for places with a Merlay look-alike name. There was only one which qualified in Normandy, so we headed for the town called Le Merlerault. This involved manoeuvring the local train system and then a cycle ride of a few kilometres.

[37] Rev John Hodgson, History of Morpeth, 1832, Frank Graham 1977, p 10
[38] Percy Hedley, Northumberland Families Vol 1, The Society of Antiquaries of Newcastle upon Tyne, 1968, p 196

We arrived at the town just before twelve o'clock as the market in front of the *hotel de ville,* the town hall, was beginning to close up. A good omen was that the emblem on the town's coat of arms contains a blackbird, *un merle,* as ours does in Morpeth.

Where would we start? The tourist information office was the obvious place, and they are usually to be found in town halls in France. In we went. There was no sign of a tourism department. The sign on the door indicated that the town hall would close at twelve o'clock. We knocked on the door to the *mairie,* the mayor's office.

We tried to explain in our modest French that we were looking for information about the possible origin of the de Merlay family who had been the first barons of Morpeth after the Conquest. The mayor's *secretaire* did his best, but it was lunchtime. He called his *maire,* and we tried again to explain to this kindly woman what we were after. Was there any historical information? Should we go to the church to see what was there? Was there a castle?

They pulled out of a filing cabinet a short historical article and copied it for us. Yes, there was a *chateau* but it was private. That was all they could find to help us.

We had a slight problem. The local hotel had closed down, and the *maire* was concerned because she didn't know how we could return to our *chambre d'hôtes* in another part of Normandy that night. Two Englishwomen of grandmother age on bicycles! What could they do with us?

We agreed that we'd visit the church to see what could be found out there, and the *secretaire* recommended a restaurant for the important midday meal. We would return to the *mairie* at 4 pm, where the *maire* said she'd help us find a place for the night.

The church was what a church had always been – a place for worship. There was no sign of any historic information, and it showed no architectural features from the early Norman period as far as we could see. This town was clearly not a tourist centre of significance. We cheered ourselves up with a three-course midday meal at the restaurant *l'Aurore,* and then explored the quiet town where everyone seemed to be having an after-dinner nap. We looked at the backs of the older houses on the main street, where the gable ends reminded us of the yards of Morpeth.

At 4 pm we returned as arranged. The *maire* had organised her son to take us to the town of Sées in his van, bicycles and all, where we could get a train to Argentan and stay in a hotel for the night. We accepted her kind arrangement, and she allowed us to take a photo of herself beside the geraniums outside her town hall before we left.

Mme Martine Gressant, mayor of Le Merlerault. An informal snapshot taken at the visit of Rosie and Bridget to the town hall

Until we got back to England, there was no more that we could find out. The historical booklet contained little of use. A few communications between us in Morpeth and the *maire* followed, but nothing definite emerged. The link with Montbray was established however, and that at least was something. With the help of my French-speaking friend Carol, a few telephone conversations between the *mairies* of Montbray and Le Merlerault followed, but it was all a little vague. Our French friends were rather bemused by these approaches. Our friendly mayor of Morpeth was very open to making contact with these Normandy towns. The trouble was that we hadn't anything definite to go on, particularly with Le Merlerault.

More than a year passed by. I was well into reading and thinking about this story. And then, as sometimes these things do, we fell across what we needed when we were least expecting it. Carol was googling Ranulph de Merlay and Le Merlerault. There was a very confusing entry in Wikipédia which among other things stated that Ranulph had founded in 1129 the abbey of Saint Cuthbert near Morpeth, in other words Durham Cathedral, and later in 1138 founded the Cistercian Abbey of Newminster. After that, the entry continued with a possible Ranulph de Merlay who went on a crusade, wanted to marry a princess Constance of Antioch, and who was assassinated in 1152 in the company of Raymond of Tripoli. None of this made any sense, except the mention of the founding of Newminster.

Despite this, the clue which solved the mystery of the origins of the de Merlays was in one of the references to this confused selection. I immediately began to google *Dictionnaire de la Noblesse*. I'm no great googler, but I got to the 1775 edition of the *Dictionnaire* and managed to find the entry for the origin of the de Merlay family. It correctly named our William de Merlay and his son Ranulph. It even mentioned William's wife Menialda.

The site wouldn't allow me to copy and paste or print the entry. I got my pencil and wrote it out on a piece of paper before anything happened and it disappeared off my screen. I had it!

Yes, the de Merlay family originated in the barony of Merle-Raoul situated between Argentan and l'Aigle. This was the right place, just where Le Merlerault is located.

Yes, William was the second son of Roger du Merle and Emma Giroye, who had married about 1050, according to Orderic Vitalis the monk chronicler.[39] They were parents of Raoul and William, our William de Merlay.

Yes, William was the father of Raoul, (another spelling of Ranulph) and Roger.

Yes, William de Merlay and Menialda (spelled as Mencalde) his wife and Ranulph their son gave land at Boremith (which was almost certainly Morwick near Warkworth) to an abbey called Saint Cuthbert of Durham.

Yes, after the death of William de Merlay, his son Ranulph confirmed this donation in 1129.

Most of this I had already been able to verify.

Yes, yes, yes, yes and yes. So now we knew for sure that the baronial family who were given Morpeth after the Norman Conquest had originated in the area around the town of Le Merlerault.

Roger, William's father, and hence Ranulph's grandfather, had been one of the knights who accompanied Duke of Normandy in his conquest of England in 1066. This was gratifying new information.

If they chose, people in the two towns could now make a friendly link.

---

[39] Orderic Vitalis, Vol 1, Bk lll, p 395. This verifies the entry in *Dictionnaire*, with one or two quibbles which may be owing to the translation.

DICTIONNAIRE

DE LA

NOBLESSE

CONTENANT

Les Généalogies, l'Histoire & la Chronologie
des Familles nobles de la France, l'explication de leurs Armes
et l'état des grandes Terres du Royaume, possédées à titre de Principautés, Duchés
Marquisats, Comtés, Vicomtés, Baronnies, &c., par création
héritages, alliances, donations, substitutions
mutations, achats ou autrement.

On a joint à ce Dictionnaire

LE TABLEAU GÉNÉALOGIQUE ET HISTORIQUE

DES MAISONS SOUVERAINES DE L'EUROPE

ET UNE NOTICE DES FAMILLES ÉTRANGÈRES, LES PLUS ANCIENNES,
LES PLUS NOBLES ET LES PLUS ILLUSTRES

PAR

DE LA CHENAYE-DESBOIS ET BADIER

TROISIÈME ÉDITION

entièrement refondue, réimprimée conformément au texte des Auteurs
& augmentée d'une TABLE GÉNÉRALE de tous les noms
de familles, de terres, de fiefs, d'alliances cités dans le cours de l'ouvrage, ainsi que d'un ARMORIAL
représentant les blasons de Maisons dont les généalogies sont comprises
dans cette édition.

TOME TREIZIÈME.

A PARIS

Chez SCHLESINGER frères, libraires-éditeurs

Rue de Seine, 12.

M DCCC LXVIII

---

*The above version is the cover from the 1868 edition.
The contents for the Merle family are the same in the
1775 and 1868 editions*

Below is the entry in the Dictionnaire de la Noblesse,
and its translation into English

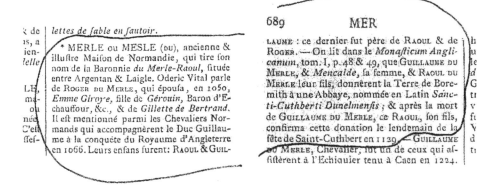

MERLE or MESLE, ancient and illustrious house of Normandy, which takes its name from the barony of Merle-Raoul, situated between Argentan and l'Aigle. Orderic Vitalis speaks of ROGER DU MERLE, who married, in 1050, Emma Giroye, daughter of Gerouin, Baron of Echauffour, etc, and of Gillette de Bertrand. He is mentioned among the Norman knights who accompanied the Duke William at the conquest of the kingdom of England in 1066.

Their children were RAOUL & WILLIAM: the latter was father of RAOUL [Ranulph] & ROGER.

One may read in the Monasticon Anglicanum, vol I, p 48 and 49, that WILLIAM DU MERLE and Mencalde his wife, and RAOUL [Ranulph] DU MERLE their son, gave the land of Boremith [Morwick] to an abbey named in Latin Saint Cuthbert of Durham; and after the death of WILLIAM DU MERLE, this RAOUL, their son, confirmed the donation the day after the fête of St Cuthbert in 1129.

William de Merlay's mother and the link with the Orderic Vitalis

Emma de Giroye was William's mother, as can be seen recorded in the *Dictionnaire de la Noblesse*. She was a daughter of William Geroie, who was one of the founders of the abbey of Evroult, the abbey to which the child Orderic was sent at the age of ten. This is where he wrote his history which we are using so frequently as evidence in this story. It is quite a pleasing thought that our William de Merlay's mother, and his grandfather, are linked with Orderic Vitalis and his abbey of Evroult in this way.

William de Merlay, Ranulph's father

The nitty-gritty of the William de Merlay evidence

In between the visit to le Merlerault and the discovery of the evidence in the *Dictionnaire,* I'd been gathering information and checking up sources. What could be found out with reasonable certainty about William de Merlay? When did he come to England? With the Conquest, or later? How did he come to Morpeth? And does it actually matter anyway?

But of course it does. This is Morpeth's fundamental history. I was anxious to get down to the nitty-gritty.

The trail involved a convoluted route backwards from the works of Northumberland's 19th century historian Rev John Hodgson. Hodgson's works are not exactly bedtime reading but he is the most invaluable source of information. There are two specific sources in his *History of Morpeth* which lead us to the origin of William de Merlay.

His first source can be picked up on page 10.

> William de Merlay, according to Leland, was a serjeant to Geoffrey, bishop of Constance, about the time of the Conquest.[40]

So William was a *serjeant* of Bishop Geoffrey. Constance in fact was Coutances, the cathedral town that my sister and I had visited in western Normandy.

On page 56 of his history, Hodgson affirmed the connection with the Battle of Hastings.

> William de Merlay also fought at Hastings, under the bishop of Constance's banner.[41]

His source for these statements was John Leland, a 16th century historian.

In another part of his work, Hodgson referred to Simeon of Durham.

> Here is a plain intimation that William de Merlay, and his patron the bishop of Constance, were in some way connected with the north of England; and it seems probable that de Merlay, before that year, 1088, either from the crown, or Mowbray, viceroy of the county, had acquired the Morpeth estate, for his services in the battle of the Conquest.[42]

The reference to 1088 concerned an important trial in which William de Merlay played a minor part, and which we'll read about shortly.

Hodgson wrote with confidence that William de Merlay, *according to Leland*, was the servant of Bishop Geoffrey. How could I know if it was true? And if it should be, how did Leland know?

There is clear evidence from a charter that William de Merlay died in 1129.[43] Thus if he had fought at the Battle of Hastings in 1066 at perhaps aged 15 which seems the youngest likely age, he would have been about 78 when he died. This is a very great age for a warrior in the circumstances of those days, but it is not impossible. So far, so good.

Hodgson didn't give a source for his Leland quote, so the first task was to find the latter's works. This was where the digging began.

Leland is best known for his travel writings called *Itineraries*, and they can be found in the shelves in the basement of the Lit and Phil library in Newcastle. I interrupted a serious student as I rummaged around on the floor, pulling out a 1907 edition from a lower shelf. But although I found other well-known quotes of Leland about Morpeth and Alnwick, I found nothing about de Merlay.

The introduction to the volumes informed me that during the five years he'd spent travelling around the country, he had copied a great number of documents many of which had been compiled into works called the *Collectanea*. There didn't seem to be anything like a *Collectanea* in the *Itineraries*.

Should I give up? Was it really that important to know?

One day I was looking at William Dugdale's *Baronage* of 1675 in the section on the de Merlays.[44] Dugdale also referred to William de Merlay's being a *servant* to the Geoffrey the Bishop of Constance. Perhaps it was where Hodgson's spelling of *Constance* had originated because he would certainly have been familiar with the *Baronage*.

And Dugdale did give a detailed reference to Leland's 1560s *Collectanea*, in volume 1, page 543.

---

[40] Constance is a spelling which has caused much confusion in the past. It is certainly Coutances. Hodgson, A History of Morpeth, p 10
[41] Hodgson, p 56
[42] As above, p 56, citing Bedford's Simeon of Durham, 1732
[43] Hodgson, p 105
[44] Dugdale, Baronage of England, 1675, p 570

There is another library in Newcastle which had a 1774 Latin copy of the *Collectanea*. With the help of kind librarians, I consulted it, but the book stopped long before page 543. I felt stumped. Was I to take Hodgson's word for it that Leland said that William de Merlay actually been a servant to Geoffrey of Coutances about the time of the Conquest?

It is the kind of thought which comes when one is day-dreaming. As there is a volume I of the *Collectanea,* there must surely be a volume 2. Off I went once more to the Newcastle library. Satisfyingly, that turned out to be the case. Again volume 2 didn't go as far as page 543, but there were section numbers in the margin, and there, in section 543, in minuscule writing, was what I wanted. The whole story hangs on this tiny little piece of evidence.

Gul: de Merleio fervus epifcopi Conftantienfis.

If we modernise the *s*, it would read:

   Gul: de Merleio servus episcopi Constantiensis[45]

   William de Merlay servant of the bishop of Coutances.

Hodgson translated the word *servus* as *serjeant*.[46] Dugdale translated it as *servant*. They both translated Constantiensis as Constance.

But how did Leland, writing in the 1560s, know this about William de Merlay? We aren't yet quite at the root of the story.

I needed to understand the context of this short Latin phrase. It was in a list in a sub-section of the *Collectanea* entitled *Ex libro summi altaris Dunelmi,* which means *From the book of the high altar of Durham.*

While all these various visits to the libraries were going on, I had been organising my notes, reading and thinking. I went again to the library to have a further look at the Latin phrase.

I have only the most minimal Latin, and was wondering who I could get to help me understand its context when I realised something significant. The phrase was in a list of names and events which appear in the account of the famous trial in which William de Merlay appeared in 1088.

The list shows a "Magna *f*uit lis inter Gul: Ru*f*um & Gul: epi*f*copum Dunelmen*f*sem", which translates as a "great quarrel between King William Rufus and William the bishop of Durham". Below that, in the list of names, was the simple abbreviated phrase showing William de Merlay.

---

[45] John Leland, Collectanea, Volume II, London 1774, p 386, margin section 543
[46] Hodgson, Morpeth, p 10

21

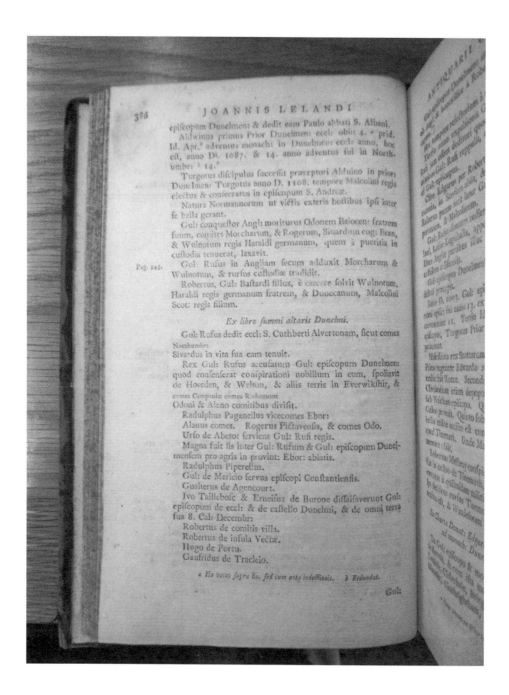

Gul: de Merleio ſervus epiſcopi Conſtantienſis *can be seen on the ninth line from the bottom.*

From Leland's 1560s Collectanea, *in volume 2, page 543.*

With thanks to the Society of Antiquaries of Newcastle upon Tyne

This and preceding photo by Denis Peel

The list of names and events is like a prompt list for a story which a person is preparing to write. The extract follows with short notes about later happenings.

The trial of 1088, the great quarrel, can be seen in an appendix to Simeon's *History of the Church of Durham,* entitled *The History of the Unjust Persecution of the First Bishop William.*[47] This is the story in which William de Merlay plays a very minor part, and from which Hodgson took the longer quote above. We will learn all about it soon. In the account, de Merlay refers to the bishop of Coutances as "my lord". Once more, we have confirmation that de Merlay served Bishop Geoffrey.

While wondering what to make of this list, and gazing dreamily at the Latin names one day, I decided to compare it with the story in Simeon's history. Yes indeed, although spelled in quite different ways, the Leland list consisted of the same people, and in the same order, as they appear in the story of the trial. You can see if you agree with me by looking at Appendix 2.

Right. Now we know that Leland's list and the story of the *Unjust Persecution* are connected. The list and the story are from the same or closely related sources, and the story was written only a matter of two decades after the trial took place, probably before 1109.[48]

What can we say that we now know for certain about William de Merlay?

We can be sure that he served Bishop Geoffrey of Coutances. Hodgson certainly thought he fought at the Battle of Hastings in 1066, and if so, he would have been a young man, hardly more than a boy, at the time. We know that he was an adult servant to Bishop Geoffrey in 1088. We do not have proof that he was old enough to fight at Hastings, although it seems most likely that he did, and the dates which we do have are compatible. If he did fight in the battle, then in the year of his death, 1129, he would have been an old man of about 78 years.

This story has led us backwards from Hodgson to Dugdale, from Leland to Simeon, all great researchers and historians. We are in immense debt to them. If Simeon or his contemporary hadn't jotted down William de Merlay's name in the list, and similarly if the writer of the *Unjust Persecution* hadn't noted William de Merlay's part in the trial, we would not know that the man who became the first baron of Morpeth had served Bishop Geoffrey of Coutances. Nearly all the rest of his story leads on from that simple piece of information, and now it is time to tell it.

---

[47] The History of the Unjust Persecution of the First Bishop William, appendix to Simeon, History of the Church of Durham, p 731. Written by an unknown monk. Also in English Historical Documents, p 621.
[48] Bernard Meeham, Symeon of Durham, ODNB, 2004 - 2015

The Book of the High Altar

The Leland extract was in a section of his *Collectanea* called *The Book of the High Altar of Durham*. A knowledgeable friend said to me: "Oh, that is the Liber Vitae, the Book of Life. It is also sometimes called *The Book of the High Altar*."

The *Liber Vitae* is an important source of verification for some of the characters we will meet in the stories which follow. It lists the important visitors to the church of St Cuthbert in Durham, from about 840 AD to 1300 AD.

But nowhere in the voluminous tomes of the *Liber Vitae* could I find the names in the Leland list.

Then, another knowledgeable friend mentioned a different *Book of the High Altar*, the *Red Book*. He pointed me to a historic tract from 1925, in which the historian H H E Craster explained that Leland had recorded a now lost document which was part of the *Red Book*.

"One is forced to the conclusion that there were two separate books kept on the high altar, and that the book … Liber Summi Altaris is untraced, and presumably has perished."

From the work of Simeon or the unknown monk, Leland had recorded this slender item of crucial importance to our story, and it once appeared in the Red Book.

Gul: de merleio ſervus epiſcopi Conſtantienſis

From Norman fields to the land of conquest

The young boy William, who would in time become Ranulph's grandfather, grew up in central Normandy, near the small town we know as Le Merlerault. Until we find out more about the subject, we know of no surviving castle or *motte* from that time. The twentieth century article given to my sister and me at the *mairie* tells us this.

> Le nom du Merlerault évoque pour l'agriculteur une region plantureuse d'élevage du cheval et du boeuf.
>
> The name of Merlerault evokes for the farmer a green and grassy place where horses and cattle are raised.[49]

Despite the lack of hard and fast information, we may permit ourselves to imagine young William and his older brother Raoul becoming accomplished riders as befitted sons of a knight, practising their skills in the fertile fields grazed by horses and cattle. The young men rode horses of a really special breed. These were the horses which William and his commanders brought on the boats of the Conquest, and which would certainly have impressed the English. They were descended from those bred by the Moors of Spain.[50]

We have confirmed that the young William was a servant of Geoffrey, the Bishop of Coutances, in the Norman conquest of England. The bishop was one of Duke William's most important followers, and appears regularly in the records which survive from those times. William de Merlay was a relatively minor player in the grand scheme of things. To discover the story that leads him to Morpeth, we will follow the trail of his famous master, and allow ourselves to picture him as an observer and participant.

It all started with Duke William in 1066.

---

[49] Dictionnaire du pays d'Argentan, Le Merlerault, 1965
[50] Graeme Ritchie R L, The Normans in Scotland, Edinburgh, 1956, p 174 notes

The call to war 1066

Duke William was summoning the great lords of Normandy and their followers. It was a call to war. He had an ambitious plan – the conquest of England.

There are three characters whose careers during the conquest would lead to William de Merlay, father of Ranulph, becoming the baron of Morpeth. Their stories inter-relate, and we will be following them. The three men are Bishop Geoffrey of Coutances, his nephew the young Robert de Mowbray, and William de Merlay himself, also a young man. Their story leads us to the arrival of the Normans in Morpeth.

We know for certain that Bishop Geoffrey and William's and Robert's fathers attended the king's call. It is possible that the two younger men did too, although we cannot be sure.

Orderic Vitalis, whom we have already met in the Gospatric story, told us what happened. Writing only fifty or so years after the Conquest, he knew people in whose memories the information was still fresh. At that time, he wrote, "Normandy was favoured by possessing many accomplished prelates and illustrious nobles."[51]

He listed seven great bishops, including Bishop Geoffrey. The most important was the better-known Bishop Odo of Bayeux, whose name is associated with the famous tapestries. He was William's half-brother, and he would also play a role in the history of Northumberland.

Orderic wrote that "foremost in the ranks of the laity" were other nobles, counts, the son of an archbishop, the duke's cousin and his standard bearer.

> There were many others whose valour had gained them military distinction, and whose native sagacity and decision in council were not inferior to the matured virtues of the Roman senate, but aspired to imitate them both in their indefatigable constancy, and the talent and courage they employed in conquering their enemies.

Roger de Mowbray, brother of Bishop Geoffrey of Coutances, was named. It is likely that William's father Roger du Merle was one of the "many others". A good number of these nobles were related to Duke William.[52] Together, they were an ambitious, energetic and warlike group.

The invasion

At the gathering of these nobles, Duke William presented his plan to invade England. Those who would go with him were taking a great risk but also would reap rewards if the invasion was successful. It was not immediately obvious that this was a good idea.

Orderic tells us about those in favour:

> All these were summoned by the duke's command to a general consultation; and upon an affair of so much importance being submitted to their consideration, opinions were divided according to the differences in men's minds. The more daring spirits, willing to flatter the duke's ambition, encouraged their comrades to plunge into the contest, and were for engaging in so great an enterprise without hesitation.

But many were more cautious:

> Others were opposed to an undertaking of so much difficulty, pointing out to those who were too venturesome, and were running headlong to destruction, its great inconveniences and perils; they magnified the obstacles presented by the want of a fleet and the dangers of the voyage, and alleged that a handful of Normans were unequal to the conquest of the numerous hosts of the English.

---

[51] Orderic, Vol 1, Bk III, p 462
[52] Orderic, as above; commentary notes by the translator Thomas Forester, Vol 1, Bk III, p 462. He specifies many who were related to the Duke, but Roger du Merle is not one of those named

Finally, Duke William sent for advice to Pope Alexander in Rome. Should he make this invasion? Who was the rightful king of England, Harold or William? The pope judged in favour of William, and sent him the standard of St Peter the apostle, "by whose merits he would be defended against all dangers".[53] The fleet of wooden boats was built by August 1066 and ready to leave. However it needed a south westerly wind and, for week after week, the tensions were building up as the would-be conquerors waited. At last a westerly wind enabled the fleet to move as far as St Valéry, a little further east. Bishop Geoffrey, Roger du Merle and perhaps young William were on the boats.

As for their families, their wives, mothers, aged parents and young children who would be left behind, it was a time of great worry.

> For the intimate friends and relations of those who were to remain at home, witnessing the embarkation of fifty thousand knights and men-at-arms, with a large body of infantry, who had to brave the dangers of the sea, and to attack an unknown people on their own soil, were moved to tears and sighs, and full of anxiety both for themselves and their countrymen.

On the 29th of September, the Norman army crossed the sea. They took possession of Pevensey and Hastings. The English King Harold had just defeated an invasion by Harald king of the Norwegians at the Battle of Stamford Bridge. He knew he would have to march south, although his army was weakened. He ignored advice from his nobles, and the concern of his mother. A king kicking his mother? That is an odd trifle of information to survive the centuries.

> Refusing to listen to words of caution, he even forgot himself so far as to kick his mother when she hung about him in her too great anxiety ... Having assembled vast numbers of the English, he led them by forced marches against the enemy.[54]

On the night before the Battle of Hastings, many of the Norman soldiers worried that this might be their last night on earth. The duty of bishops was to care for their eternal life, and Bishop Geoffrey of Coutances had an important and recorded role.

The Norman poet Wace told the story in the French of the day, writing about one hundred years after the event.[55] First he described the raucous behaviour of the English soldiers.

> On Eve of the Battle, as I have heard tell,
> The English held Wassail, and feasted them well;
> Carousing and drinking through all the Night long,
> Their whole Camp re-echoed to riot and Song.
> "Drink home! and find Courage, ye faintest of heart,
> "To face the Sword's edge, or the point of the Dart.
> "Drink home! for if this be the last Cup we drain,
> "We revel in Death, if to-morrow we're slain."
>
> Quant la battaille dut joster, la nuit avant, ço oï conter,
> Furent Engleiz forment haitiez, mult riant è mult enveifiez;
> Tote nuit mangierent è burent, unkes la nuit el lit ne jurent.
> Mult les véiffiez demener, treper, è faillir è chanter;
> Bublie crient e weissel e laticome e drincheheil,
> Drinc Hindrewart e Drintome, drinc Helf e drinc Tome.

The pious French soldiers however prayed and confessed.

> Whilst Normans and French, till the morning grew grey,
> With Priests and with Friars deep Orisons said,
> Confess'd them, bewail'd their offences, and pray'd.

---

[53] Orderic, Vol 1, Book III, p 463
[54] Orderic, Vol 1, Book III, p 482
[55] Wace, The Conquest of England, from Roman de Rou, translated Alexander Malet, London, 1860, Bell and Daldry, pp 116 – 119

And who found no Priest his confession to take,
Took care a clean breast to his Comrade to make.

E li Normanz è li Franceiz
Tote nuit sirent oreisons, e furent en aflicions.
De lor pechiez confez se sirent, as proveires les regehirent,
E ki n'en out proveires prez, a son veizin se sist confez.

We may assume that Wace was painting a biased picture of the hooligan English and the pious French to flatter his patrons.

Bishop Geoffrey de Coutances and Bishop Odo of Bayeux heard the prayers and confessions of the soldiers.

The Bishop of Coutances, whose name was Giffrei,
With blessing, strict penance on many did lay,
The like did brave Odo, the Duke's brother, do,
Who held in the Vessin, the See of Bayeaux.

Giffrei, Eveske de Constances, a plusors joint lor penitances;
Cil reçut li confessions, e dona li bénéiçons.
Cil de Baieues ensement, ki se contint mult noblement;
Eveske su de Baessin, Odes aveit nom, filz Herluin.

The coronation
As we all know, the Norman invaders were victorious. Harold, the king of England, was killed. Duke William of Normandy and his army made their way to London where the duke had himself crowned king on Christmas day.

Bishop Geoffrey played an important part in the coronation at Westminster.

The king-to-be entered the doors of the cathedral, which were guarded by a line of Norman horsemen. All seemed peaceful. Everything had been prepared inside the church, a new crown rich with jewels was ready, and a crowd of spectators, both Norman and English, filled the minster. First came the clergy carrying the cross, then the bishops, and then surrounded by his chief supporters Duke William himself.

The ceremony needed to be conducted in two languages.

> When Aldred the archbishop was demanding of the English, and Geoffrey, bishop of Coutances, of the Normans, whether they consented to have William for their king, and the whole assembly loudly gave their willing assent, with one voice though not in one language, the men-at-arms, who formed the guard outside the abbey, upon hearing the shouts of joyful acclamation raised by the people in the church in a language they did not understand, suspected some treachery and imprudently set fire to the neighbouring houses.

> The flames quickly spreading, the people in the church were seized with panic in the midst of their rejoicings, and crowds of men and women, of all ranks and conditions, eagerly struggled to make their escape from the church, as if they were threatened with some immediate danger … They … hastened to the scene of conflagration, some to make vigorous efforts to extinguish the flames, and more in the prospect of committing robberies in the confusion that prevailed.

> The bishops only, with some few of the clergy and monks, maintained their post before the altar, and trembling with fear completed the coronation office with some difficulty, the king himself being much alarmed.[56]

We can see from this how close Bishop Geoffrey was to the new king of England, which would have significance for young William in due course.

---

[56] Orderic, Vol 1, Bk III, p 491

Merlay follows the military bishop

In the years following the coronation, Bishop Geoffrey was very active in the service of King William. His military and administrative talents were put to good use. There was much to do and many battles to be fought. Not all of the English had accepted the new king. We have seen the resistance to his rule in the north. Most of the activities of Bishop Geoffrey were however in the south. In 1069, at the time of the harrying of the north and Gospatric's rampagings in Cumberland, Bishop Geoffrey had been leading a military force on the king's behalf, at Montacute castle in Somerset.

> At that time the West Saxons of Dorset and Somerset and their neighbours made an attack on Montacute, but by God's providence they were foiled in their attempt; for the men of Winchester, London and Salisbury, under the command of Geoffrey, bishop of Coutances, came upon them by surprise, slew some of them, and mutilating a number of the prisoners, put the rest to flight.[57]

The bishop moved back and forth between England and Normandy in the course of his duties, signing charters in both places.[58]

Orderic summarises his personality.

> This bishop prided himself on his noble birth, and was more distinguished for his skill in war than his knowledge of divinity; better able to array men-at-arms for battle, than to instruct cowled clerks in the chants of the church. He was, therefore, often engaged in conflicts with the English and Danes, and when the enemy was subdued, obtained vast possessions, which, at his death, he bequeathed to his nephew Robert Earl of Northumberland.[59]

Like the other significant nobles and warriors who had followed the duke, Bishop Geoffrey was hugely rewarded with lands in England. There were two main groups of estates. The western group consisted of 76 estates in Somerset, 97 in Devon, 10 in Gloucestershire, eight in Wiltshire and two in Dorset. The eastern group consisted of 28 estates in Northamptonshire, 17 in Buckinghamshire, 12 in Bedfordshire, seven in Oxfordshire, two in Huntingdonshire and one in each of Leicestershire, Berkshire, Lincolnshire and Warwickshire. Many other properties and fees supplemented these estates, and historians have calculated that he was the seventh richest baron in the country, after the king and his two half-brothers.[60]

These estates were in the south of England, and later we will read about their importance to our story when they were inherited by the future earl of Northumberland.

William de Merlay would have been deployed as the bishop decided. There does not appear to be any certain evidence, but the historian le Patourel, who has studied the life of Bishop Geoffrey, offers one possibility. Some of the eastern group of estates were held directly by the bishop, rather than tenanted out, and he had a steward called William. Le Patourel writes that it "would be pleasant to know" if this man was the "William de Merlao", the servant of the Bishop of Coutances.[61]

---

[57] Orderic, Vol 2, Bk IV, p 26
[58] John le Patourel, Geoffrey of Montbray, Bishop of Coutance, English Historical Review, 1944, pp 148 – 150
[59] Orderic, Vol 3, Bok VIII, p 17
[60] Patourel, p 152, citing Corbett, Cambridge Medieval History
[61] Patourel, p 153

Why would a bishop wield a weapon of war in a battle?

Orderic, Vol 2, Book IV, pp 49-50

"What shall I say of Odo, bishop of Bayeux, who was earl palatine, and generally dreaded by the English people, issuing his orders everywhere like a second king? He had command over all the earls and barons of the realm, and with the treasures collected from ancient times, was in possession of Kent … The character of this man, if I am not deceived, was a compound of vices and virtues; but he was more occupied with worldly affairs than in the exercise of spiritual graces.

"Geoffrey, bishop of Coutances, was of an ancient Norman family, who rendered essential services and support at the battle of Senlac [Hastings], and was a commander of troops in other conflicts, in which natives and foreigners crushed each other."

Historian Everett Crosby explained a little more.

"Bishops of this period were often great landholders, drawn from noble families who were under an obligation to provide a certain number of armed men when called upon by their lord. Having led them to battle, it was not difficult for the war-minded to take up arms as well … the chief problem is to decide, in a given instance, whether the prelate accompanied the troops and encouraged them with his prayers and sermons, or whether he actually wielded sword, lance and shield."

Crosby, *The King's Bishops,* Appendix II, p 286.

Bishop Odo, left, wielding a club at the Battle of Hastings

The text may be translated as "Bishop Odo holding his staff encourages the lads"

ODO EPS BACVLV TENENS CONTOR *is above, and* TAT PUEROS *below the horse to the right*

Illustration from the Bayeux Tapestry replica at Reading Museum, who also kindly supplied the translation

The harrying of Northumbria   **1080**

Bishop Odo of Bayeux is now poised to enter our story. The north of England was not yet under the new king's control. After he drove Gospatric I into exile in 1072, the king appointed Waltheof, son of the former earl Siward, as earl of Northumbria. Waltheof joined another revolt against the conqueror which failed, and Waltheof was beheaded. Bishop Walcher, the man whom Gospatric had earlier escorted to Durham in 1071, was then allowed to buy the earldom.[62]

But once again Northumberland suffered a Scottish incursion. In 1079, Malcolm III invaded.

> Malcolm of Scotland came into England with a great army, ravaged Northumbrian land up to the Tyne, killed many hundreds of men, and took home much money, many treasures, and men in captivity.[63]

It wasn't long before Walcher was murdered by rebellious Northumbrians at Gateshead. He was lured into a trap, and he and all his retainers were killed when the church in which they had hidden was burned.

It was over a decade since the Battle at Hastings, and the king was losing patience. He took his revenge once again. He sent Bishop Odo of Bayeux, his half-brother, to the north, and this time the harrying went further than Yorkshire. Here are two extracts from Simeon.

> In retaliation for this horrible murder, king William the same year ravaged Northumbria; sending thither Odo, bishop of Bayeux, with a large military force.[64]

and

> Odo, bishop of Baieux, who was second only to the king, and many of the chief nobles of the kingdom, came to Durham, with a large body of troops, and, in revenging the bishop's death, they reduced nearly the whole land into a wilderness. The miserable inhabitants, who, trusting in their innocence, had remained in their homes, were either beheaded as criminals, or mutilated by the loss of some of their members. False accusations were brought against some of them, in order that they might purchase their safety and their life by money.[65]

The historian Kapelle has interpreted these events.

> Odo's purpose seems to have been to kill Northumbrians. The Normans slaughtered and maimed both the guilty and the innocent, and they were apparently able to weaken the native nobility seriously, killing or driving into exile many of its members.[66]

After that, and determined to do something about further threats from Scotland, King William sent his son Robert into Scotland in 1080 with an army to counter King Malcolm. The Scottish king declined to fight. After meeting at Falkirk, and following negotiations, Robert returned through Northumberland. On its way north, and then again on its way south, the army trampled over the countryside.

When the king's son Robert reached the Tyne on the return journey, he organised the building of a castle on the north bank of the river. Newcastle became the base from which the Norman kingdom would defend its gains. What lay to the south was fairly secure. The new castle was looking north, beyond Morpeth, towards Scotland.[67] This part of Northumberland was not yet fully under the Norman yoke.

A strong leader was needed to stabilise this unsettled situation, a Norman upon whom William could rely. A decade and a half after the Norman conquest of most of England, Robert de Mowbray comes riding his warhorse into our story.

---

[62] Kapelle, p 137
[63] Anglo Saxon Chronicle, English Historical Documents, p 159; Savage, p 212;
[64] Simeon, Kings, p 152
[65] Simeon, Church, p 699
[66] Kapelle, p 141
[67] Kapelle, p 141 - 142

Robert de Mowbray, Earl of Northumberland   1085 - 1095

Proud, dark and crafty

> Robert, son of Roger de Mowbray, was distinguished for his great power and wealth; his bold spirit and military daring caused him to hold his fellow nobles in contempt, and inflated with empty pride he disdained obedience to his superiors. In person he was of great stature, size, and strength, of a dark complexion and covered with hair, his disposition bold and crafty, his features melancholy and harsh. He reflected more than he talked, and scarcely ever smiled when he was speaking.[68]

That is how Orderic described the man who would become the new earl of Northumberland. The name de Mowbray is found in street names in Morpeth and other parts of Northumberland, and yet how little most of us know about him. His career is part of the chain of events which would bring William de Merlay to Morpeth.[69]

The king's first choice as earl however had been a Norman called Albric. He was yet another man who seemed unable to master the troublesome borderland, as Simeon pointed out.

> The king then gave that honour to Albric, who being of very little use in difficult affairs, returned to his country; and the king gave the earldom of Northumberland to Robert de Mowbray.[70]

Bishop Geoffrey of Coutances may himself have been first made earl of Northumberland after Albric. There are two references to Geoffrey in a charter of the foundation of St Mary's Abbey at York in 1089 recorded by William Dugdale.

> Godefridus Constantiensis episcopus, qui eo quoque tempore Northanhumbrorum consulatum regebat.

and

> About this time Geffrey, Bishop of Coutance, had of the Government of this Earldom; for being one of the Witnesses to the Foundation Charter of S. *Maries* Abbey at York, it is said.[71]

Bishop Geoffrey certainly had influence in the north. It is possible that he spoke on his nephew's behalf to King William. Hodgson thought so.

> It is certain that Geoffrey, bishop of Constance, in Normandy … fought on the side of William the Conqueror, at the battle of Hastings; and was nominated earl of Northumberland, after the murder of Walcher, bishop of Durham, in 1080, but contrived to have that office conferred upon his nephew, Robert de Mowbray.[72]

Robert de Mowbray became the earl at some point during the 1080s. There is uncertainty about the exact date, and differences of opinion among historians. Bishop Geoffrey may have been acting as earl in 1089, according to the above suggestion. Percy Hedley writes that Robert became earl in 1082, and the historian Richard Lomas writes that it was probably about 1085 which is the date I'll be using here.[73]

There is no surviving record of the young Robert de Mowbray being active during the Conquest or in England immediately afterwards, although he may well have been. He was a close ally of King William's son Robert who would become Duke of Normandy after his father's death, and had accompanied him into temporary exile from Normandy in 1078. Two decades after 1066, he

---

[68] Orderic, Vol 3, Book VIII, p 17
[69] There is no surviving record of the young Robert de Mowbray being active during the Conquest or in England immediately afterwards as far as I know, although he may well have been. He was a close ally of King William's son Robert who would become Duke of Normandy after his father's death, and had accompanied him into temporary exile from Normandy in 1078. Orderic, Vol 2, Book V, p 173
[70] Simeon, Kings, p 144
[71] Dugdale, Monasticon Anglicanum, 1665, Vol 3, p 546; Dugdale, Baronage,1675, p 570
[72] Hodgson, p 56
[73] Hedley, p 145; Richard Lomas, County of Conflict, Tuckwell, 1996, p 12

was a battle-hardened warrior. This proud, brooding, dark and silent man became the earl of Northumberland.

I find myself wondering how much prior knowledge Robert de Mowbray had of the north when he took over the role of earl. As a close colleague of Robert of Normandy, he may have accompanied him on the invasion of Scotland although I have found no record of this. The new castle on the Tyne and the great fortress at Bamburgh were both in his acquired earldom.

One of his most important tasks after he was appointed as earl in or around 1085 was to establish baronial strongholds against Scottish invasions into Northumberland, Durham and Yorkshire.[74] The Wansbeck crossing was one such place.

Merlay stronghold on the Wansbeck
It may be taken for certain, wrote historian Percy Hedley, that earls were appointed by the king, and that barons were appointed by the earls at this period.[75]

In this way, KIng William appointed Robert de Mowbray as earl, perhaps influenced by his close supporter Bishop Geoffrey, and de Mowbray would have appointed William, the bishop's *serjeant,* to the barony in Morpeth.[76]

As the second son of his parents Roger and Emma, William de Merlay had become a man of influence. His older brother, Raoul, would probably have inherited the estate back home in Normandy. Now William had a barony of his own in the newly conquered land.[77]

Once established in Morpeth, William de Merlay had an important job to do. Twenty years after the Conquest of 1066, he would establish his castle on a strategic high point near a ford over the river Wansbeck.

He was one of the earliest Normans to be established in Northumberland and to build a castle north of the Tyne. Historian Richard Lomas explains.

> It is safest to assume that between 1080 and 1095 the Normans occupied, but did not settle in, what was to be Northumberland. The one possible exception is Hubert de la Val, who may have been granted an estate by Earl Robert … In fact, only two Normans apart from Hubert de la Val have a serious claim to have been settled in Northumberland before 1100: William de Merlay at Morpeth and Guy de Balliol at Bywell. The others almost certainly came during Henry I's reign [1100 – 1135].[78]

William de Merlay and his followers, perhaps with Earl Robert de Mowbray and his men, would have arrived on horseback, armour clanking, together with their foot-followers, to the river crossing. The first thing to do was to build the new Norman-style stronghold, a motte and bailey castle. The motte was the mound, and the bailey an enclosed surrounding area.

They chose a site on a ridge of land between the River Wansbeck and the stream which is now called Postern Burn. They needed to heighten the hillock to make the motte. To do this, it looks like they dug a ditch on the western side, thus cutting into the ridge. They used the material from the ditch to steepen and heighten the selected site.[79]

The whole process was a substantial task. The labour force had to be assembled from among the bewildered and unwilling local people who had to be organised and fed. It would take quite some time, and exactly how long is not entirely clear. Once the motte had been built, the timber

---

[74] Kapelle, p 142 - 148
[75] Hedley, p 19
[76] Hodgson, Morpeth, p 10 citing Leland
[77] G W S Barrow, The Anglo-Norman Era in Scottish History, A Land for Younger Sons, Clarendon, 1980, pp 1-29
[78] Richard Lomas, County of Conflict, Tuckwell Press, 1996, p 15
[79] Historic Environment Record 11068/8 provides a detailed description of the procedure. Also C Hunter Blair, The Early Castles of Northumberland, Archaeologica Aeliana, 4th Series, 1944

tower and encircling walls had to be constructed. Chroniclers wrote that King William the Conqueror took eight days in 1066 building Dover castle, and Orderic gave the same length of time for the second castle at York. In their book, *Timber Castles*, the authors query these records.

> What exactly did they mean? Surely the entire sites could not have been completed? The most probable explanation is that a defensible perimeter, quite possibly prefabricated, could be created in such a time, together with a minimum of accommodation. The other building operations no doubt dragged on and on.[80]

We can only imagine how the new Norman lord of Morpeth, William de Merlay, would have rounded up the local people into gangs, and forced them to help with the digging of the ditch, the raising of the motte and sawing of the timbers. We can wonder at this initial encounter between the local families who had survived so much misery already and the foreigners, the shouted orders in the incomprehensible French, and the resentment of the labourers as they dug into the earth and moved the barrowloads.

The Bayeux tapestry has an illustration of men at work building a timber castle. At the scene of the construction of the castle at Hastings, workmen are industriously shovelling up earth to build the motte in layers. There is a timber palisade constructed on the summit.[81]

Constructing a motte, with the timber tower on its top.
AT HESTENGA CEASTRA *may be translated as "Castle at Hastings".*

Illustration from the Bayeux Tapestry replica at Reading Museum, who also kindly supplied the translation

In castles like this, which the Norman invaders built throughout the land that they had conquered, the bailey was the surrounding guarded outer area. The palisade defending the bailey was made of a row of sharpened wooden timbers. Our familiar Northumbrian word *pele* may come from the word *palisade*. Inside the bailey, the new Norman baron would gradually organise construction of the workaday buildings including stables, bakery, barns and carpenters' workshops.

Morpeth's motte is the unmistakable dome of Ha' Hill, a prominent landmark to this day. We don't know for sure where the bailey was constructed. One archaeologist suggests that it was on the small hill to the west, and another that it was more likely to be to the east in the area of the formal flower gardens, the Turner Garden and the aviary, between the motte and the present

---

[80] Robert Higham and Philip Barker, Timber Castles, Batsford, 1992, p 136
[81] Higham and Barker, p 155

main road.[82] Wherever it was, nothing remains of it to this day, whereas at Elsdon, in the Northumberland National Park, a well preserved motte with its bailey has survived.

Elsdon motte, with the bailey in the foreground being grazed by sheep. The photo is taken from its surrounding rampart, and there would have been a bridge connecting the two.

There is no record of what Morpeth's first castle looked like. However a monk called Laurence described the timber castle built only a few years earlier at Durham. Morpeth's might have looked something similar, though perhaps it was not quite so grand.

On this open space, the castle is seated like a queen; from its threatening height, it holds all that it sees as its own. From its gate, the stubborn wall rises with the rising mound, and rising still further, makes towards the comfort of the keep ... a stalwart house springs yet higher than the keep, glittering with beauty in every part; four posts are visible, one post at each strong corner ... The keep holds out the charm of a round appearance, pleasing in its craft, its elegance, its posture.

[the bailey] ... contains goodly habitations. There you will find two vast palaces built with porches .. the chapel stands out supported on six pillars ... Here chambers are joined to chambers, house to house ... here are fine costumes, there shining vessels and flashing arms, here money, meat and bread. Here is fruit, there wine, here beer, there a place for fine flour ... A wall goes to the plain where the youth often held their joyous games.[83]

The motte on Ha' Hill as it can be seen today

[82] Historic Environment Record 11068, sources 8,9,10
[83] The monk Laurence, cited in Higham, p 118 - 119

Once the castle was built, we can assume that it was continually guarded, and that William de Merlay used it for his *caput honoris,* the headquarters of his barony. We have no proof, but it pleases me to picture it as the home of William's family, which Ranulph and Juliana would occupy in their turn.

William marries Menialda

At some point, William de Merlay married Menialda. Who was she? Was she an English woman, or was she a Norman? Her name is mentioned in a charter which we'll see shortly. The couple had four children, three sons and a daughter, Ranulph, Goffrid, Morel and Eustorcia.

In the 1080s, when Northumberland was still recoiling from the devastation caused by the Scottish invasions and the harrying of Bishop Odo, life was very uncertain. Did the couple marry after William de Merlay became the baron of Morpeth, when perhaps his life was beginning to settle down? Had he already married? We do not know, but the dates table at the front of this book has included some possible dates for the marriage and the birth of their children.

Although Morpeth was his headquarters, William probably moved around a good deal in the service of his master Bishop Geoffrey and Robert de Mowbray. Menialda and the children would be left at home.

Earl Robert de Mowbray's church at Tynemouth

As for Robert de Mowbray, after he was appointed as earl in or around 1085, things may have been settling down a little.

> The daily activities of men such as Earl Robert de Mowbray in the wilds of Northumberland were not gaudy enough to attract the attention of the chroniclers, and nothing is known … Outside the ecclesiastical sphere between 1080 and 1087, according to the chronicles, there were no murders, revolts, or invasions, and Norman power was uncontested, at least during daylight hours and away from the woods.[84]

The cathedral at Coutances built by Bishop Geoffrey in the 11th century

With kind permission of Association des Amis de la Cathédrale de Coutances

---

[84] Kapelle, p 146

Earl Robert however had a big ambition. He wanted to build a new church. My own suspicion is that he wanted one comparable with his uncle's famous cathedral at Coutances which he was sure to have seen as a young man.

Tynemouth, in his new earldom, was the site he chose. The earlier church there had belonged to the monks of St Cuthbert at Durham but by the 1080s it had fallen into a state of disrepair. After disagreements with the bishop of Durham, Earl Robert transferred the church to the monastery of St Albans in Hertfordshire. He may have developed contacts there during the many years of his activities in the south with Bishop Geoffrey.

Earl Robert's church at Tynemouth was of a rare design in England but common in Normandy. It had an apse, a round passage behind the choir and the altar. The aisles circling around behind formed a passageway known as an ambulatory, through which worshippers could walk.[85] Although much enlarged later, there is still some evidence of Earl Robert's original building.

Some parts of the earliest church at Tynemouth, dating back to the time of Earl Robert de Mowbray, can still be seen in the rounded Noman arch

When Abbot Paul of St Alban's was visiting his monks who were established at Tynemouth, he was taken ill. On his way home he died. Simeon considered that this was just retribution for the way Earl Robert had taken Tynemouth from its rightful owners at Durham.[86]

> There appeared a wonderful sign in the sun … Paul, abbot of the monastery of St. Albans, died. This Paul, having by the aid of earl Robert taken possession of the church of Tynemouth, contrary to the injunction of the monks of Durham, for it belonged to them, was there attacked by illness; and on his journey home, he died at Seterington near York.[87]

It is certain that William de Merlay would have known about Earl Robert's prestigious new church, and I can imagine him chatting with Menialda, and thinking about an equally important establishment for his own barony. The fulfilment of that ambition would have to wait until their son Ranulph grew up, and their new daughter-in-law arrived at Morpeth.

Rebellion in the south west   **1088**
William the Conqueror died in 1087 and the crown of England was in dispute. Another rebellion was about to take place. Earl Robert de Mowbray, the new earl of Northumberland, and his militaristic uncle Bishop Geoffrey would be off to battle again.

---
[85] Craster, H H E, Northumberland County History, Vol VIII, p 136
[86] Simeon, Kings, 1093, p 159; Simeon, Church, 1083, p 704. Historians debate the date of this episode.
[87] Simeon, Kings, p 159

King William had declared that his elder son Robert, the same who had built the castle at Newcastle, should become the duke of Normandy, and that his second son William should become king of England. King William Rufus was crowned in September 1087.

Both Bishop Geoffrey and Earl Robert de Mowbray supported the claim of Robert of Normandy to be king of England. They were among the group of great Norman barons who held substantial properties in both Normandy and England.

Very likely William de Merlay, with his close connections to the bishop and the earl, took part in the rebellion. William de St Calais, Bishop of Durham, was also involved.

Simeon of Durham told the story.

> In 1088, a dissension arose among the nobles of England; for a small part of the Norman nobility favoured king William, the other and the greater number were in favour of Robert, earl [ie duke] of the Normans … The leaders in this infamous affair were Odo, bishop of Bayeux, who was also earl of Kent; Geoffrey, bishop of Coutance … [many others are listed]. They secretly concocted this execrable plot during Lent, and immediately after Easter began to ravage all around … Geoffrey, bishop of Coutance and Robert de Mowbray went to Bristol, where they had a very strong castle, and they laid waste the entire country as far as the place called Bath.[88]

The chronicler Florence of Worcester gave some more details.

> Having burned and plundered Bath, they passed on towards Wiltshire where he [Earl Robert de Mowbray] ravaged the vills and slaughtered many of the inhabitants, and at length reached Ilchester, and sat down before it, determined to take it … but … Robert, being repulsed, retired, mourning over his ill success.[89]

It is hard to sympathise with Robert's mourning after he and his uncle the bishop had destroyed the vills and slaughtered many of the helpless peasants.

Ultimately the rebels were unsuccessful. The warrior bishop Odo, who had ravaged Northumbria in 1080, was defeated by King William Rufus, and the rebellion was at an end.

---

[88] Simeon, Kings, pp 154 - 155
[89] Florence of Worcester, p 189 (His works are now believed to be by John of Worcester)

Odo was banished, but the king came to an agreement with many of the rebels. Earl Robert de Mowbray, Bishop Geoffrey of Coutances and William de Merlay were not deprived of their positions. The king still seemed to need their help in controlling his large and unwieldy kingdom. But they were not quite out of trouble.

William de Merlay addresses the king   1088

There was a "great dispute" in 1088 between King William Rufus and William de St Calais, the bishop of Durham. We may remember the reference to this in Leland's and Simeon's evidence concerning William de Merlay as the servant of Bishop Geoffrey of Coutances.

King William Rufus had been infuriated at the treachery of the bishop, and called him to trial at Salisbury in the south of England. Bishop Geoffrey of Coutances and William de Merlay were also summoned.

Simeon's account of the trial, the *History of the Unjust Persecution of the First Bishop William*, is many pages long. Bishop William was accused by the king of participating in the rebellion, who demanded that he give up his castle at Durham. The bishop refused the legitimacy of the king's trial, and demanded that he should be tried in an ecclesiastical court.[90]

At a certain point, our William de Merlay spoke out for his master Bishop Geoffrey. The event is of very limited importance in the trial, but it provides us with the evidence that we need.

It appeared that the king had given a safe-conduct to the passage of 200 of Bishop Geoffrey's cattle. The bishop of Durham's servants had captured the animals and refused to pay for them. William de Merlay requested that the king should require the bishop of Durham to pay for the animals.

> Then William 'de Merlao' rose and said to the king: "My lord, before the bishop came to this court, his men robbed my lord, the bishop of Coutances, of two hundred head of cattle which were in your keeping; and my lord, the bishop of Coutances, asked that they might be restored to him, but this was refused. Afterwards, Walter 'de Haiencorn', acting on your instructions, ordered that the restoration should be made, and still it was refused. Now therefore we pray you that you will cause the cattle of my lord to be restored.
>
> "You may judge for yourselves, barons," said the king, "whether I justly accused this bishop or not."
>
> But [archbishop] Lanfranc interposed: "It would be unjust if you now accused him further, because now he no longer holds any land from you."[91]

As the king was taking away the Bishop of Durham's castle and lands, he no longer had the means to pay. Archbishop Lanfranc helped him decide the issue, and the matter was then dropped.

It is very hard for us to understand the subtleties of the changing loyalties from such a long time ago. Perhaps King William Rufus was feeling baffled when he turned to the barons. He was probably worn out after the long hours of the trial.

This is a short and relatively insignificant episode in the long description of the trial. The bishop was sent into exile, where he remained for three years as one of the most important supporters of Duke Robert of Normandy. However, it confirms that William de Merlay was the servant of the bishop of Coutances, and that he was still in the bishop's service in 1088. That was twenty-two years after the Conquest, and around the time that his barony at Morpeth was established.

---

[90] Simeon, Church, appendix, The History of the Unjust Persecution of the First Bishop William, translated 1855 Joseph Stevenson, Llanerch reprint 1993, pp 731-749. For the Merlay extract, see p 746. The story also appears in English Historical Documents, p 621

[91] This version is taken from English Historical Documents, p 665. It appears as an appendix in Simeon, Church, p 746

It also emphasises the way men and animals moved with apparent ease around the country. Bishop Geoffrey seemingly had animals moving through the county of Durham. Certainly it seemed that he and William de Merlay travelled between the north and Salisbury at the king's request without difficulty.

Bishop Geoffrey of Coutances dies in Normandy   1093
In 1091, Bishop Geoffrey retired to Coutances in Normandy where he had established his cathedral early in his career. He grew steadily weaker.

He died on 2 February 1093, aged about 65.[92] His importance was shown by the powerful assembly at his deathbed, which included Bishop Odo of Bayeux, Bishop William de St Calais of Durham and many important abbots, a painting of which is on the church wall in the village of Montbray in Normandy.[93]

Earl Robert kills the king of Scotland   1093
At his death, Bishop Geoffrey left his nephew, Robert de Mowbray, his vast properties in the south and west of England. Thus Robert, Earl of Northumberland, became one of the most powerful barons in England. The inheritance would have given him a sense of his own extraordinary importance and perhaps invulnerability.

One of his tasks as earl as we saw earlier was to control the Scots. Simeon summarised the previous invasions of King Malcolm III.

> Once in King Eadward's reign … and … a second time in the reign of King William when he pillaged Cleveland … thirdly when he went as far as the Tyne, and returned with great spoil after massacring the men and burning the dwellings … fourthly he went with his numberless forces to Chester-le-Street … where a military force caused him to speedily retire from fear.[94]

In November 1093, King Malcolm III invaded once again. Malcolm was outraged by insults which had been inflicted on him by King William Rufus. This time, however, he had a formidable opponent in the new earl of Northumberland. Robert de Mowbray's troops were waiting in ambush, and they killed both the Scottish king and his son.

> The fifth time he invaded Northumbria with as large an army as he could collect, intending to bring upon it utter desolation; but he was cut off near the river Alne, with his eldest son Eadward, whom he had appointed heir of the kingdom of Scotland after him. His army either fell by the sword, or those who escaped the sword were carried away by the inundation of the rivers, which were then more than usually swollen by the winter rains. Two of the native Englishmen placed the body of the king on a cart, as none of his men were left to commit it to the ground, and buried it at Tynemouth.

His wife, Queen Margaret, was so distressed at hearing this that she fell into an illness and died three days later. Simeon considered that right had been done.

> In his death the justice of an avenging God was plainly manifested; for this man perished in that province which he had often been wont to ravage, instigated by avarice; for five times he had wasted it with a savage devastation, and carried captive the wretched natives to reduce them to slavery. [95]

The man who actually killed the king was Morel, Earl Robert's nephew who was acting as his steward. Here are the words of the Anglo Saxon Chronicle.

> Robert, the eorl of Northumbria, trapped the king of Scotland with his men unawares and killed him. Morael of Bamburgh killed him, who was the eorl's steward and king Malcolm's spiritual brother.[96]

---

[92] Patourel, p 133
[93] Patourel, p 158
[94] Simeon, Kings, p 159
[95] Simeon, Kings, pp 159 - 160
[96] Savage, p 230; English Historical Documents, p 171, translates Morael as King Malcolm's "gossip", ie one of them had acted as sponsor to the other's child, or they had both stood sponsor to the same child.

The Norman poet Gaimar also pointed the blame on Morel. He wrote his *Lestorie des Engles* in French, in or around 1136.[97]

> When the king had held his court
> The news arrived
> That Malcolm was slain,
> The king who was his enemy.
> Robert de Munbrai had killed
> This king, whether it was right or wrong.
> At Alnwick was the battle.
> Three thousand men in all by tale
> Were slain there with Malcolm;
> And on both sides many a good baron.
> It was Geoffrey de Gulevent,
> He and Morel his kinsman,
> Who took the life of Malcolm.

> Quant li reis out sa curt tenue
> La nouele li est venue
> Ke Malcolumb estait oscis,
> Li reis ki ert ses enemis;
> Robert de Munbria laueit mort,
> Cel rei, v fust a dreti, v fust a tort,
> A Alnewic fu la bataille,
> Treis mil homes trestuz par taille
> I out oscis od Malcolum,
> E de ambes parz maint bon baron.
> Co fu Gefrai en Gule went,
> Il e Morel vn son parent,
> Ki Malcolumb tolirent vie. [98]

Morel's role in this death was controversial. Gaimar writes "whether it was right or wrong". The "wrong" probably referred to the fact that Morel and King Malcolm were "sworn brothers". This "brotherhood" was a vow made in a church on the relics of a saint, and was in fashion among Normans and the Northumbrians of the time.[99]

Capture of Morpeth castle   1095
Not long after this, Earl Robert's arrogance led him to disaster.

King William Rufus had dealt rather leniently with the barons following the 1088 rebellion, as we have seen. Consequently, plots and conspiracies were always likely to happen. In 1095, many of the rebels rose up once again, and this time the leading figure was Earl Robert de Mowbray.

The rebels still weren't happy with King William Rufus, and this time seemed to want his cousin, Stephen of Aumale, a nephew of William the Conqueror, to be king. Many powerful barons were part of the conspiracy. They held castles all across England, in Suffolk, Hastings, Yorkshire and Shrewsbury. In Northumberland, Earl Robert de Mowbray held Tynemouth, Bamburgh and probably Newcastle, and his ally William de Merlay held Morpeth.[100]

King William Rufus had information about the conspiracy, and he also knew that help for the rebels might be coming from Normandy. He was ready for a confrontation, and an opportunity soon presented itself.

---

[97] Ian Short, Oxford Dictionary of National Biography, 2004-15, p 1
[98] Gaimar, Lestorie des Engles, p 259 - 260
[99] Ritchie, p 15
[100] John Beeler, Warfare in England: 1066 – 1189, Cornell, 1966, p 66 and onward

Early in 1095, Earl Robert and his nephew Morel seized four Norwegian merchant vessels. Orderic is the source of the story.

> Four large ships, called canards, sailed from Norway to England, and falling into the hands of Robert and his nephew Morel and their retainers, the peaceable merchants were stripped with violence of all they possessed. Having lost their goods, they went to court and in deep distress laid a complaint of their injuries before the king.

King William Rufus ordered Robert to restore all that he had stolen, but he refused. The king then summoned Robert to his court at Windsor, but again met with a refusal. Enough was enough. The king gathered together his army and marched north.

> The king being satisfied of the perverse temper of this fierce baron, collected troops and led a strong force against him.[101]

On the way north, he was warned by a certain Gilbert of Tunbridge that an ambush was waiting for his army in a wood a little ahead. Gilbert was one of the powerful rebels who was having second thoughts. Thanks to this warning, the king avoided the ambush and proceeded north.

> He besieged the castle of Earl Robert, which stood at the mouth of the river Tyne, for two months. During this siege he reduced a small fort in which he took nearly all the earl's best soldiers and put them into confinement; he then stormed the besieged castle itself, and committed to close custody the earl's brother, and the knights he found in it.[102]

This extract is taken from Florence of Worcester, and historians have different views about whether the castle was at Newcastle or Tynemouth. The name of Morpeth now enters history. In the excerpt above, there is also a mention of a "small fort". Could it be Morpeth?

The Anglo Saxon Chronicle doesn't name it, calling it simply "a fort".

> As soon as he came there [Northumbria] he overcame nearly all the best of the eorl's court in a fort, and put them into captivity.[103]

Simeon calls it "a certain outwork".

> During that time, having stormed a certain outwork, he took almost all the earl's best soldiers, and placed them in confinement.[104]

Historian John Beeler explains.

> In the meantime the king had captured another castle, referred to by Symeon as a *munitiuncula* and by the English chronicles as a *faestene,* which the earl had garrisoned with the pick of his troops. This was probably William de Merlay's castle at Morpeth, which had to be taken before the way could be opened to Robert's final refuge at Bamborough.[105]

Beeler's explanation is probably taken from the poem of Gaimar.

> Then the king took Morpeth, a strong castle,
> Which stood on a hill.
> Above Wansbeck it stood.
> William de Morlei held it.
> And when the king had taken this castle
> He advanced into the country.
> At Bamborough upon the sea
> He made all his host stay.

---

[101] Orderic, Vol 3, Bk Vill, pp 18-19
[102] Florence (John) of Worcester, p 200
[103] Anglo Saxon Chronicle, Savage, p 232
[104] Simeon, Kings, p 163
[105] Beeler, p 68

> Puis prist Morpathe, vn fort chastel
> Ki iert asis sur vn muncel;
> Desur Wenpiz assis estait,
> Willame de Morlei laueit.
> E quant il out cel chastel pris,
> Auant alat en cel pais;
> A Baenburc desur la mer
> Son ost ad fet tut arester.

Gaimar's poem about the taking of the castle in 1095 is the earliest historical mention of the name of Morpeth, and the castle on the hill by the Wansbeck, as far as I have been able to find out.

In this story I am accepting Gaimar's version of Morpeth being the place of the "small fort". Although the other chroniclers don't name it, Gaimar must have had some knowledge that the fort was at Morpeth, that it was next to the Wansbeck and that it was held by William de Merlay. How he knew these facts we don't know but someone, somewhere, must have told him.

Thus William de Merlay's castle played a significant part in the rebellion. Earl Robert's most important knights were gathered there, even though it is described as just a "small fort". There must have been a large enough bailey area for the knights and their horses to be accommodated, and all adequate services to cook for them and to attend to their needs. The servants and staff, as well as William de Merlay's own family members, would all be busy looking after this gathering of knights.

Doubtless the defenders had resisted the king, but the castle was taken, and the knights rounded up. In these modern days, it is hard to imagine that dramatic and terrifying event around the quiet motte in Morpeth. William de Merlay and Menialda were probably married by this time and had small children, the oldest of whom was Ranulph. William de Merlay was sure to have been among the captured soldiers.

Earl Robert's grisly end   1095
Once Morpeth was subdued, the king's army moved north to attack Earl Robert who was defending himself in his castle at Bamburgh.

Orderic gives us a glimpse of the landscape at Bamburgh in those days.

> That fortress being impregnable, the marshes and waters and other impediments to a march with which it is surrounded, rendering it inaccessible, the king caused a new fortification to be erected … and to shut in the enemy, and placed a garrison in it well supplied with arms and provisions.

Some of the knights who had been originally part of the rebellion, like Gilbert of Tunbridge, realised the weakness of their position and changed to side with the king. The new fortification was a temporary siege castle with the intriguing nickname of *Malvoisin* or *Yfel nebhur*, which means Evil Neighbour. This overlooked the castle where the earl was holding out.

> The king now held his troops ready for battle and compelled his officers and the other English nobles to urge forward the new fortification.

> Meanwhile Robert saw from his battlements, in deep tribulation, the works which were being carried on against him, and called loudly to his accomplices by name, publicly recommending them to adhere faithfully to their traitorous league to which they had sworn. The king and his faithful adherents only laughed at Robert's speeches, while the consciousness that their guilt was discovered tormented the conspirators with fear and shame.[106]

The siege looked like it would go on for a long time. Eventually, Earl Robert escaped from the castle and was captured. Here is Gaimar's version of the story.

---

[106] Orderic, Vol 3, Bk VIII, chap XXIII, pp 19-20

And many assaults he endured there.
But the castle had scant victuals;
When the earl saw that they failed,
Towards the sea by the postern …
He put to sea, he had a right good wind.
To Tynemouth he went.

E maint assaut i endurad;
Mes el chastel out poi vitaille.
Quant li quens veit de co la faille,
Deuers la mer, par la posterne …
Si se mist en mer, mult out bon vent.
A Tinemue en est alez.

Orderic's version is slightly different.

> Robert de Mowbray, disgusted and wearied with the long blockade came out by night, and attempting to pass from one castle to another, fell into the enemies' hands.[107]

The way in which Robert de Mowbray was captured varies in different chronicles. Whereas Gaimar has him leaving by sea, others explain how he was tricked on an overland flight.

Here is Florence of Worcester's account.

> The wardens of Newcastle promised earl Robert to give him admission into the fortress, if he could come by stealth. Joyfully accepting this proposal, he set forth one night with thirty troopers to accomplish his design. On discovering this, the knights who kept guard against the castle of Bamburgh went in pursuit and despatched messengers to inform the garrison of Newcastle of his departure. In ignorance of these movements, Robert made his attempt on Sunday, but the enterprise failed because it was anticipated. He therefore took refuge in the monastery of St Oswin, [Tynemouth] king and martyr, where, on the sixth day of the siege, he received a severe wound in the leg while he was resisting the enemy, of whom many were killed and many wounded. Of his own men some were wounded and all made prisoners; he himself fled to the church from which he was dragged forth and delivered into custody.[108]

Now that Earl Robert was captured, his days of good fortune were over. The castle at Bamburgh nevertheless had still not surrendered. Matilda, Earl Robert's wife, and Morel, his nephew, were holding out. But because the blockade could continue indefinitely with the seaward side being hard to control, the king decided to put an end to it. He'd been to Wales, and then returned to Northumberland where he resorted to an unpleasant measure. He would have the earl blinded if the defenders would not open the gates.

> He ordered earl Robert to be taken to Bebbanburgh, and his eyes to be put out, unless his wife and his relative Moreal should surrender the castle. Compelled by this necessity, they delivered it up; the earl was taken to Windsor, to be placed in close confinement.[109]

There is a final story about the journey of Robert de Mowbray on his way to imprisonment in the south. Simeon has a story from 1121, when a Yorkshire knight called Arnold de Percy testified that he had seen de Mowbray as he was taken through Durham.

> When the earl was taken prisoner at the place which he had seized from St. Cuthbert and was brought to Durham in a litter, on account of the wounds which he had received, he begged that he might be allowed to enter the church to pray; this not being permitted by the barons, he burst into tears, and looking towards the church, he exclaimed: "Oh holy Cuthbert, I justly suffer these calamities, because I have sinned against thee and thine; this is thy vengeance for my iniquity. I pray thee O saint of God, have mercy on me."[110]

---

[107] Orderic, Vol III, Bk VIII, chap XXIII, p 20
[108] Florence (John) of Worcester, p 201. Also see Beeler p 69
[109] Simeon, Kings, p 163
[110] Simeon, Kings, p 189

This story doesn't feel re-assuring. Robert de Mowbray was a formidable character, and picturing him with tears of repentance seems unsatisfactory. The historian Craster reports some sources which say that he ended up as a repentant monk at St Albans where he died at an advanced age and was buried.[111] Like his Northumbrian predecessor Gospatric, after a life of violence, both were reported by monk chroniclers as repenting as death approached.

As for Morel, he is one of the less pleasant characters in our story. Once he and Robert's wife Matilda had been forced to give up the castle he tried to save himself by revealing the names of the other conspirators to the king.

The Anglo Saxon chronicles report the tale.

> Morael became one of the king's court; through him were many revealed, both clerical and lay, who were in their counsel unfaithful to the king.[112]

Orderic Vitalis puts it this way.

> As for Morel, when his lord was condemned to perpetual imprisonment, he fled from England in great trouble, and wandering through many countries grew old in exile, poor and detested.[113]

Thus Morel, nephew of the earl, lost his position in Northumberland and the lands which went with it. He ended his life in exile and dishonour.

Gaimar has a few lines about the last days of Robert de Mowbray.

> He [Rufus] did not put him to death nor kill him,
> But he was in prison for twenty years.
> In the prison he ended, dying.
> A good man he became before he died.
> He never saw again anything that he had.
>
> Nel ad defeit ne nel oscist,
> Meis en prison fu puis vint anz,
> En la prison finat moranz.
> Prodom deuint ainz kil morust;
> Ia ne veiast rien kil eust. [114]

Other lesser persons in the rebellion had punishments varying from death, mutilation, fine, forfeiture or exile. It is worth noting that King William Rufus imprisoned rather than executed Robert de Mowbray. It could be that Robert still had many powerful supporters, and the last thing the king wanted was more restlessness. Orderic explained.

> The king adroitly discovered this, and consulting his counsel pardoned persons of that class. He was unwilling to bring them to a public trial, lest their exasperation should be increased, and they might be provoked to a general rising against the government, and much loss, destruction, and grief should be occasioned to the community.[115]

After this rebellion, King William Rufus decided that there would be no more earls of Northumberland. He would take control through the appointment of a sheriff directly accountable to himself.

Once Robert de Mowbray was cooped up in his prison in 1095, the link between his name and the county of Northumberland ended.

---

[111] Craster, NCH Vol VIII, p 54
[112] Savage, p 233; English Historical Documents, p 172
[113] Orderic, Vol 3, Bk VIII, p 21
[114] Gaimar, p 195
[115] Orderic, Vol 3, Bk VIII, p 22

William de Merlay must have been one of those rebels who were pardoned by the king. He and Menialda his wife and their children survived, and his family's lordship at the Morpeth barony continued.

Was the unpleasant Morel a Morpeth man?
One of the four children of William and Menialda was called Morel, and he was probably the youngest of their three known sons.[116] Percy Hedley raises the possibility that there could have been a family relationship between the de Merlay and the de Mowbray families.[117] Could Robert de Mowbray's nephew Morel have been William and Menialda's youngest son, the black sheep of the family, a Morpeth man?

The reasoning against this is that Morel must have been a fully grown man by 1095. As the youngest son of William and Menialda, he would need to have been born by about 1075. At this time, William de Merlay was still following the banner of Bishop Geoffrey of Coutances, and though it is not impossible, it is unlikely that he and Menialda had married and produced three children by this date.

However, the unusual nature of the name, which Hedley points out, means that there may indeed have been a family connection, one son perhaps being named after another older relation. We have no evidence that Robert de Mowbray and William de Merlay were related, but it is not out of the question. And incidentally, while cycling around Normandy, my sister and I often found the name Morel over shopfronts. Perhaps we have more connections there yet to be discovered.

Matilda, Lady of Bamburgh

Not much fun being wife of the hairy earl
Simeon has told us that Matilda, Earl Robert's wife, looked after Bamburgh castle along with Morel after his capture. Matilda was the daughter of an important Norman family. She had only been married to Robert for three months before the 1088 rebellion. If Robert had been a young man at the time of the Conquest, he would have been well into his forties by the time of her marriage, and she was probably little more than a girl. We will remember his description as a large, dark-complexioned and hairy man, who scarcely ever smiled.[118]

Orderic explained the reason for the marriage.

> In order to extend his territories, and that he might strengthen himself by alliances with the most powerful of his countrymen connected with him by ties of affinity, Robert married a noble lady who was daughter of Richard de Laigle, and niece of Hugh, earl of Chester, by his sister Judith.

> Matilda his wife, who had never enjoyed happiness with him, because their union was contracted at the very moment of the insurrection, and she had been led to the nuptial couch only three months before, trembling amid the clash of arms, was soon deprived of the consolations of marriage, and long exposed to deep suffering.[119]

Poor Matilda. Being led to the nuptial couch seems bad enough. Imagine then her feelings when her new husband Robert was displayed before the walls of her castle at Bamburgh. Surrender or he will be blinded in front of you, she was told. Of course she would surrender.

Once Robert de Mowbray was securely behind the walls of his prison far away in the south of England, all his lands were confiscated by King William Rufus. The properties he had inherited from his uncle, Bishop Geoffrey of Coutances, were passed by the king to Nigel d'Aubigny, a knight who had accompanied King William I on the Conquest.[120] These lands were not in Northumberland but in the south of England and in Normandy.

---

[116] Hogson, p 105, see the charter in Col I
[117] Hedley, pp 196 - 197
[118] Orderic, Vol 3, Bk VIII, p 17
[119] Orderic, Vol 3, Bk VIII, p 20
[120] Dugdale, Baronage, p 122

Nigel d'Aubigny wanted more than just Robert de Mowbray's lands; he wanted his wife as well. In the way of these inter-related Norman families, Earl Robert was Nigel's cousin. Robert's father, Roger, and Nigel's mother, Avicia, were brother and sister.[121] They would have played together in the fields of Montbray as children in the years before the Conquest.

Whether the newly married Matilda liked it or not, Nigel wanted her. But there was a problem. Robert de Mowbray was still living, and thus Matilda was not a widow. If Nigel wanted her, she needed a divorce. Influence had to be used. Orderic explains.

> Her husband lived in prison, and during his life she could not according to the law of God marry again. At length, by licence from Pope Paschal, before whom the case was laid by learned persons, after a long period, Nigel d'Aubigni took her to wife, and for some time treated her with respect, out of regard to her noble parents, but on the death of Gilbert de Laigle her brother, Nigel craftily sought a ground of divorce, and repudiated her because she had been his cousin's wife, and then he married Gundrede ... [122]

Having married Matilda knowing that she was his cousin's wife, he then repudiated her on the same grounds. The couple had not had any children and thus he wanted to be rid of her. Matilda's brother Gilbert must have been a powerful protector of his sister, and his death gave Nigel the chance to reject her.

In 1118, during the rule of King Henry I, Nigel obtained his divorce and then married Gundrede. She was the daughter of the powerful Norman de Gournai family, and sister of the earl of Surrey.[123] Whether or not she trusted her new husband to treat her better than he had treated Matilda we cannot know. She would certainly have thought about it. Together they had a son whom they called Roger. Adding insult to injury to Matilda, by a special command of the king he was given the name of Roger de Mowbray.[124] When he grew up, he became a significant figure in the later history of England. But as the lands he inherited are not in Northumberland, the name de Mowbray passes out of our story.

We don't know how Matilda's life ended, but Orderic's translator noted that she owned estates in the counties of Dorset and Stafford which paid Danegeld in 1130.[125] As Robert de Mowbray reportedly lived for thirty years after his capture in 1095, it looks like she outlived him, and I hope that she found some happiness.

The marriageable value of heiresses
Heiresses owed service of marriage throughout their lives. Fifty was a good old age for men, and most died younger either in battle or of disease. A girl, married in childhood, might be free to marry many times and each time she was widowed she would have a right to dower for life, which was a factor to be considered by prospective suitors and therefore increased her "market" value to her lord.

O G Tomkeieff, p 53

No more troublesome earls

After he had destroyed the power of Earl Robert in 1095, King William Rufus appointed Robert Picot as sheriff, based at Bamburgh and responsible directly to the crown. There would be no more troublesome earls.

The strength of the Scottish kings to invade Northumberland was weakened after de Mowbray had killed King Malcolm III in 1093. In 1097, Edgar, a son of Malcolm III, became king of Scotland. He remained loyal to the Norman kings of England.

---

[121] Orderic,Vol 3, Bk VIII, p 21, notes
[122] Orderic, Vol 3, Bk VIII, p 21
[123] Orderic, Vol 3, Bk VIII, p 21, notes
[124] Dugdale, Baronage, p 122
[125] Orderic, Vol 3, Bk VIII, p 21, notes

In 1100, after the death of William Rufus in a hunting accident, his brother Henry, the youngest son of William the Conqueror, took the throne of England.

Soon after Henry became king, William de Merlay made an important donation.

The Morwick charter

William had to take care of his eternal soul. He was becoming old, and death approached. Knowing how he had fought and killed his way to his barony, the prayers of holy men might ease his path through purgatory. Like many Norman barons, he decided to donate some of his land to the church, and he chose the cathedral of St Cuthbert at Durham. The charter recording the donation in Latin can be seen in Hodgson's *History of Morpeth* and in the *Monasticon Anglicanum.*[126] Here is my version in English.

> I William de Merle, with the agreement of my sons and my wife, give to God and the holy saint Cuthbert, and the monks of Durham, Morwick with all that belongs to that vill, and as well a fishery in the Tyne, for my soul and for my wife Menialde, and for my sons Ranulph de Merle, and Goffrid, and Morel, and all my other sons.
>
> + Sign of William de Merle. + sign of Ranulph his son. + sign of Goffrid his son. + sign of Morel his son. + sign of Robert. + sign of Anser de Merlei. + sign of Goffrid of Clifton, freely and peacefully, in perpetual alms.

In his *Baronage of England,* Dugdale states that the grant was in the time of Henry I.[127] It could be about 1110, at which time William and Menialda's three sons, Ranulph, Goffrid and Morel could have been about 17, 16 and 15 years of age, old enough to put their crosses to a charter. Noticeably, none of them could write.

Ranulph de Merlay was growing up in his family castle beside the Wansbeck, and Juliana was no longer a mere child playing beside the sea. The events which would link them together were unfolding further. Our story now moves to the rocky headland at Dunbar, to the castle in the land of the exiled Gospatric family.

---

[126] Hodgson, Morpeth, p 105; Dugdale, Monasticon Anglicanum, 1817 edn, p 241
[127] Dugdale, Baronage, p 570

Above: The rocky headland at Dunbar, the surrounding shore and the remains of the medieval castle today. This could have been the playground of the young Juliana and her brothers

Gospatric II, Juliana's father

> Dunbar castle stands a short distance north from the town in a situation particularly wild and romantic. It is founded upon a reef of rocks that project into the sea, and which, in many places, rise like bastions thrown up by nature to guard these stern remains of feudal grandeur against the power of the waves, that yet force their way through rugged caverns and fissures in the stone, and, with a thundering noise, wash its dark foundations.[128]

James Millar, *History of Dunbar*, 1859

Juliana's childhood

Growing up in a castle, perched on a rocky reef overlooking the sea, with rocks to climb on and waves to leap over, sounds like every child's ideal playground. Juliana and her brothers Gospatric III, Waldeve, Edgar and Edward would have spent their childhood clambering, splashing, collecting shells, fishing, and sometimes dreaming of faraway places they might reach in a boat, north to Dunfermline to the palace of the king of Scotland, south to their ancestral Northumberland, or further away to England. Their father would tell them about their grandfather who had joined the Danes from across the sea and his other battles when he fought the Norman conquerors.

Of course really we don't know for sure if the children did live there. Still, Dunbar is the place to which Gospatric I came after his exile in 1072, and believed to be the site of the family castle. Historian Elsa Hamilton has written about the earliest known ruins.

> The present red sandstone ruins of the castle of Dunbar are perched, precariously to the eye, on a rocky outcrop some fifteen metres above the sea ... this is not the fortress which Gospatric would have occupied when he came north in the eleventh century. Within the ruins, fragments remain of an earlier castle ... it may be that the fragmentary remains belong to a twelfth or thirteenth-century castle. In that case, an even earlier structure of red sandstone or wood must have stood on the rock, and this would have been the stronghold to which Gospatric came.

It is also possible that the centre of defence was not actually on the rock where the present castle stands, but on the headland immediately above.[129]

While Juliana was playing around the castle, and no doubt causing her mother Sibilla plenty to worry about, her father Gospatric II was frequently away in the service of the king of Scotland. The family were by no means desolate, living in what was once part of the ancient kingdom of Northumbria, an area which they would consider to be rightly their inheritance. Still, the loss of Northumberland would have been painful. Those fertile, productive fields, the rolling hills and the woodlands where the deer could be hunted, would be missed and longed for.

Scottish kings		English kings	
Edgar	1097 – 1107	William Rufus	1087 - 1100
Alexander I	1107 – 1124	Henry I	1100 – 1135

The king of Scotland at the time of Juliana's childhood was Edgar, son of King Malcolm III who we will recall had been killed in 1093 by Robert de Mowbray's nephew Morel, near Alnwick.

After Edgar died in 1107, his brother Alexander succeeded him as king. Juliana's father Gospatric II was a loyal subject of both the Scottish kings who themselves were close to the king of England. In 1100, Henry I had taken the throne, and the same year he married Matilda, Edgar and Alexander's sister. This close connection between Gospatric II and the kings of Scotland, and hence the king of England, had an influence on Juliana's life.

---

[128] James Miller, The History of Dunbar, 1859
[129] Hamilton, pp 24 - 25

Matilda and Juliana were both descended from King Ethelred of England (978 – 1016), of the fifth generation in descent through their different lines. Each girl would have known this important fact, and Juliana would surely have known that she was related to the girl who became the queen of England.

Queen Matilda of England lived at Westminster where she welcomed many creative and literary people including foreigners "who spread fame of her munificence far and wide".[130] Her mother, Queen Margaret of Scotland, had had a reputation for her love of colourful fabrics, and for endowing the church with beautifully embroidered vestments and gold and silver vessels.[131]

These influences were part of the culture in which Juliana's father Gospatric II moved, and which would be brought into the family home. One of the few surviving stories about Gospatric II is that he was a witness to the charter of King Alexander's inauguration of the priory of Scone.[132]

> Alexander came in state and, with all his lords around him, "in witness and token" of the gift, made his men bring up to the altar "his comely steed of Araby", richly caparisoned, his "costly armour of Turkey … and shield and spear of silver white".[133]

Of course Gospatric II would have told his wife and daughter about this event. He was probably one of the lords around the king.

The new King Henry needed security in the borderlands between England and Scotland, and Gospatric II wanted his family earldom of Northumberland back. The young girl playing in the waves at Dunbar was growing up. She could be part of a bargain.

The first thing Gospatric II needed to do was to negotiate which lands Henry might pass to him, and what he would be expected to do in return. The close links between the kings of Scotland and England may have eased the process. Henry and Gospatric reached an agreement, and it was recorded in a charter at some date early in Henry's reign, probably before 1111.

At the same time as Gospatric II was looking out for his family's interest, William de Merlay at Morpeth would be doing the same. He needed a wife for his son Ranulph, and why not a girl who would bring some more land to his rather modest barony? His castle controlled a river crossing in Morpeth on one of the main routes between England and Scotland. An alliance with a family who held lands along that route would be likely to be useful to King Henry. The two families acting together could control rebels or highwaymen.

---

[130] Ritchie, p 126
[131] Ritchie, p 78
[132] Greenwell, p 104
[133] Ritchie, p 172

And so it was done. First, a lands charter was settled, and then in a second charter Juliana's father and King Henry agreed that Juliana should marry into the de Merlay family. Her future was being arranged.

The lands charter   c 1110

Gospatric II didn't get all the land that he would have wanted, but he received a lot.

The original lands charter which would tell us about it is unfortunately lost, but there is a confirming one from about 1135 made at York by King Stephen in about 1135. It can be seen transcribed in the Percy Cartulary, easily available in Newcastle libraries.[134]

It starts with greetings from King Stephen.

> I, Stephen, king of the English, send greetings to the justices, barons, sheriffs, ministers and all the faithful of Northumberland, both French and English. You should know that I have given and granted to Gospatric, brother of Dolphin … [135]

THE PERCY CHARTULARY.   333

DCCCXI. Stephanus[1] rex Anglorum, justiciis et baronibus et vicecomitibus et ministris et omnibus fidelibus suis, Francis
et Anglis, de Northumbreland, salutem. Sciatis me reddidisse[2]
et concessisse GOSPATRICIO FRATRI DOLFINI terram Edmundi,
advunculi sui, quam de rege Henrico tenebat, et terram
WINNOCHI, videlicet, sex maneria, BREMDONAM, et BENELEGAM,
et HIDDESLEIE, et BREMETONAM, et THITELITTONAM,[3] et HAROP,
cum omnibus hominibus et rebus que fuerunt in terra illa die
qua rex Henricus dedit illa maneria Hamoni. Et terram
Liolfi filii Octredi, videlicet, tres MIDELTONAS, et RODEN,[4] et
HORSELEIAM, et servicium Gospatrichii, et STANTONAM, et
WYNDEGATAM, et WOTTONAM, et (folio 125 d.) WITTONAM, et
RITTONAM,[5] sicut rex Henricus ei illas dedit et concessit per
cartas suas. Et habeat suas rectas divisas quas monstrare
poterit se juste habere debere. Et ideo volo et precipio quod
bene et in pace et honorifice et libere et quiete teneat pre-
dictas terras suas et omnia sua, in bosco et plano, et pratis, et
pasturis, et aquis, et molendinis, et stagnis, et exclusis, in via[6]
et semitis, in divisis et exitibus, et in omnibus locis, cum socha
et sacha, et tholl et theam et infangthef, et cum omnibus
libertatibus et consuetudinibus suis, sicut melius unquam
tenuit et liberius tempore regis Henrici, et super hoc omnes
fugaciones que feodo suo pertinent. Testibus, R. canc' et
W. Mart', et R. de Veer,[7] apud Eboracum.[8]
   DCCCXII.[9] Libertates Novi Castri super Tynam. De
tallio dando et accipiendo apud Novum Castrum, tempore

It goes on to describe three blocks of land.

The first was that part formerly held by Gospatric II's Uncle Edmund. Who was he? Perhaps he was the brother of Gospatric I's wife whose name we don't know. Here is a hint that some of the Gospatric lands, linked to the family through marriage, may have been retained from the time of exile. The townships of which this block consisted were not named at this time, but a later charter informs us that they were Shipley, Edlingham, Lemington and Learchild.[136]

A second block was the land of Winnoc the hunter. The townships were named as Beanley, Brandon, Hedgeley, Branton, Titlington and Harehope.

---

[134] Percy Cartulary, Surtees Society Vol 117, 1909 - 1911, p 333; also see Greenwell, pp 31 – 34. In this charter, Gospatric is described as *Gospatricio Fratri Dolfini*, meaning *Brother of Dolphin*, who would thus be Juliana's uncle
[135] With thanks to Gail Boyes
[136] See the charter of Earl Patric II of Dunbar, Newminster Cartulary p 268

The third was the land of Liulf, comprising ten townships. They were three Middletons with Roddam in the north of the county, and what is of particular interest to us, a separate set of townships some miles further south, nearer to Morpeth. Between the Coquet and Wansbeck rivers, these were Horsley, which we now know as Longhorsley, Stanton, Wingates, Wooton and Witton which we now know as Longwitton and Netherwitton, and Ritton.[137]

The lands which were being returned to the family became known collectively as the *serjeanty* of Beanley. Henry placed particular conditions on the grant. Gospatric II was required to control the roads passing between England and Scotland. The service required was known as *inborwe and utborwe,* or in other spellings as *inborg and hutborg,* or *inbourgh et outebourgh.*

> The true meaning of this service seems to be that the owner of the fee should act as insurety and outsurety for the peaceful and honest intention of persons passing to and fro between the two countries, who would not be allowed to travel therein without permission from the holder of Beanley to do so.[138]

Gospatric II, in his fastness at Dunbar and as possessor of land in Northumberland, would be in an ideal position to control the routes between the two countries.

The townships on the map are those named in the charter of King Stephen above, together with some other lands held by Gospatric II in Bewick and Eglingham from the monastery of St Albans. He didn't have those lands for nothing.[139] He had to pay rent of £4 a year to the monks of Tynemouth, who held it from St Albans, plus either 20 shillings or seven oxen each with a value of three shillings.[140]

What the map clearly shows is the strategic importance of Henry's donations. An important north south route was the Devil's Causeway, a former Roman road which may still have been in use at that time. A little west of Morpeth, the route passed through the townships of Netherwitton and Horsley. Further north it passed through the townships of Edlingham, Lemington and Learchild, and further north again through Beanley, Branton and Brandon. From near Beanley there were several routes heading north towards Scotland. The Devil's Causeway continued to the Tweed just south of Berwick, with land and sea connections to the Gospatric castle at Dunbar. Other routes led towards towards Wooler and Wark where new baronies were being established by Henry I. Having a *serjeant* supervising movements along those routes would be very useful for Henry.

The lands were granted by King Henry to Gospatric II with all proper boundaries and rights including "soc and sac, toll and theam, and infangthef".[141] These terms meant that Gospatric had the rights to hold a court and expect tenants or vassals to attend; to receive tolls which could be lucrative if they controlled the through-routes; to hold a market; and to try and even hang thieves.[142] Although Gospatric II had not inherited the role of earl in Northumberland, some restitution had been gained.

In the castle at Dunbar, more comings and goings would be observed by Sibilla and Juliana. Messengers would be passing along the roads between Morpeth and the River Tweed, and from there to Dunbar. King Henry, Gospatric II and William de Merlay were making another agreement.

---

[137] Percy Cartulary, p 333, note
[138] Greenwell, pp 30-31
[139] For further details, see Colm O'Brien, p 60
[140] Greenwell, p 32.
[141] Greenwell, p 30
[142] Domesday Book, A Complete Translation, Penguin 1992; Joy Bristow, The Local Historian's Glossary of Words and Terms, Countryside Books, 2001

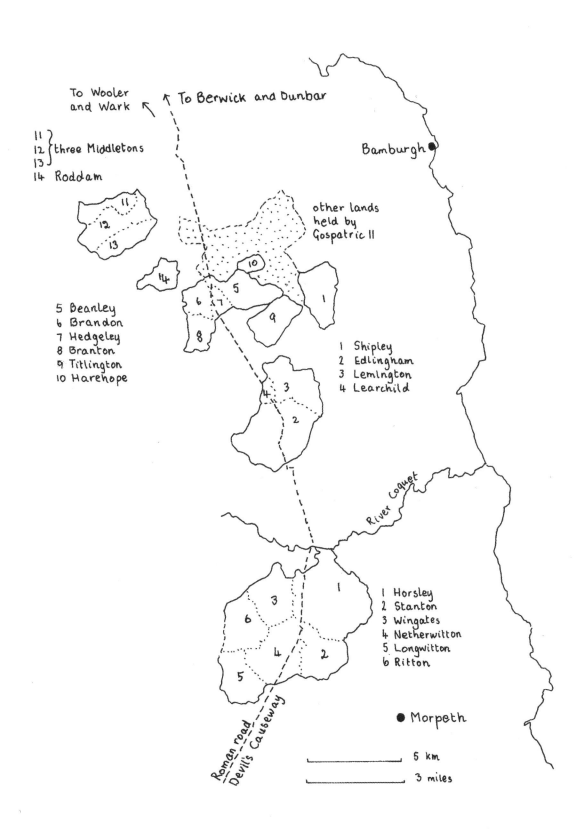

To Wooler and Wark

To Berwick and Dunbar

Bamburgh●

11
12 } three Middletons
13
14 Roddam

other lands
held by
Gospatric II

5 Beanley
6 Brandon
7 Hedgeley
8 Branton
9 Titlington
10 Harehope

1 Shipley
2 Edlingham
3 Lemington
4 Learchild

River Coquet

1 Horsley
2 Stanton
3 Wingates
4 Netherwitton
5 Longwitton
6 Ritton

●Morpeth

Roman road
Devil's Causeway

5 km

3 miles

Lands donated to Gospatric II by King Henry I in the early 1100s

Townships on the map

The boundaries shown on the map here and later are based on *townships*, also known as *vills*. They weren't villages so much as traditionally-bounded areas of land with settlements which could be small villages or dispersed houses, and would include cultivation, meadows, woodland, moorland waste and commons. These townships were already in existence at the time of the Norman conquest, and are likely to be those named in the charters.

Boundaries once established are often long lasting. Historian Piers Dixon has calculated that about 75% of the medieval townships in north Northumberland are closely related to the civil townships mapped by the Ordnance Survey in the 1860s, which are those I am using in this book. See his work *The Deserted Villages of North Northumberland*, p 79, available at Northumberland Archives.

Another expert landscape historian Brian Roberts uses the same source. He writes that the boundaries of the Ordnance Survey maps of the mid-nineteenth century while by no means definitive are of substantial antiquity and create a necessary framework for all historical research, p 64 notes. Also see Northumberland National Park's Historic Villages Atlases, chapter 3.

The marriage charter   c 1112

The king had ruled. No-one could deny it. Juliana was to be married according to his wishes, with the agreement of her father, to one of his Norman barons. We don't know for certain her age, but she may have been about 15, the marriageable age for both girls and boys at this time.[143] Her marriage charter starts with the words of the king.

> Henry, king of England and Duke of Normandy, to the justiciaries, vice-counts, ministers and all his barons, French and English, of Northumbria, salutations.
>
> Be it known to all of you that I have given to Ranulph de Merlay in free marriage Juliana, daughter of count Cospatric ...[144]

The right of the king to decide who Juliana might marry seems extraordinary from our modern perspective. However, he was in fact keeping on the better side of his barons by making some concessions. When he was crowned, he had agreed to loosen some of the royal powers, recorded in what became known as his Coronation Charter. Clause three included this paragraph.

> If any of my barons or of my tenants shall wish to give in marriage his daughter or his sister of his niece or his cousin, he shall consult me about the matter; but I will neither seek payment for my consent, nor will I refuse permission, unless he wishes to give her in marriage to one of my enemies.[145]

The Coronation Charter was circulated to every shire in England. Both Juliana's and Ranulph's parents would know this clause. Gospatric need not pay the king a fee, and equally he could choose his daughter's husband, within reason.

Here is a full modern translation.

> Henry, King of England and Duke of Normandy, to all his ministers and barons, both French and English, of Northumbria, greetings. Let it be known to all of you that I have given Juliana, daughter of count Cospatric, to Ranulph de Merlay.

---

[143] Bitel, p 165
[144] See note below for translation information
[145] English Historical Documents, Coronation Charter, p 400

You should also know that because of [an agreement] between me and her father we have given to her and to her heirs, in free marriage, the following: Horsley, Stanton, Wittton, Ritton, Wyndgates, and a certain vill beyond the moors. They are to be held as freely as anyone is able, more freely between spouses or to give to someone else in their demesne.

And for this matter I command my justices to see that nothing is lacking, and if anyone wants to argue against it then I command my justices and sheriffs of Northumbria to do full right to it.

Testibus, Patricio fil., Joha. Peuerell de Baelcamp', Willelmo de Allunbrito, Henr. fil. Johannis, Willelmo del Pont del Harche, Willelmo Maltrauar', Willelmo Maldut, apud Wodstok.[146]

She would bring to her marriage the townships of Horsley, Stanton, Witton, Ritton and Wingates, and the village across the moors which we know from other sources to be Learchild. These townships can be seen on the map above. With the exception of Learchild, these places were all very close to Morpeth and near the de Merlay barony. Her dowry was certainly a useful addition to the prestige and power of her new family.

Juliana's marriage agreement, from the Castle Howard archive, as it now survives. Our graphics artist has underlined the words Henricus Rex Angl' et Dux *along the top line.*

Also see Edgarus Gospatri comitis filius *at the beginning of the top line of the second paragraph, and underneath that, the words* Julianae sorori meae. *Details about Edgar's charter follow below.*

Reproduced with kind permission of the Howard family.

---

[146] Translation by Gail Boyes, with guidance from Teresa Saunders. The last paragraph has been left in Latin owing to uncertainties caused by the punctuation. For Latin versions, see Appendix 3 from the Newminster Cartulary pp 268-269, Hodgson, Morpeth pp 106 – 107, and Monasticon Anglicanum, 1846 edition, Vol 5, Folio item 271 – 1, p 399. The full marriage charter is printed out in Appendix 3

Gospatric II's plan for a take-over

It looks like Gospatric II was positioning himself for a gradual recovery of land in Northumberland. The townships of her dowry were never "incorporated with the de Merlay barony" but "continued to be held by the Cospatric serjeanty of Beanley", as Hodgson pointed out.[147] I'd always wondered what that meant. In some way, Gospatric II was ensuring that his family held some power over the de Merlays. But how?

Elsa Hamilton's book gave me some clues. Like Hodgson, she wrote that the lands which Juliana "brought to her marriage with Ranulf de Merlay, lord of Morpeth, were never incorporated into his barony, and continued to carry the obligation of service to the Dunbar earls."

Obligation of service? What was that? Elsa Hamilton gave some references about this service which I was able to track down in a Newcastle library.

There were three extracts from legal disputes concerning this obligation. Once again, it is necessary to go to a later time and look backwards. In 1263, the descendants of Juliana and Ranulph, by this time Earl Patric III of Dunbar and Roger de Merlay III, were squabbling in court.

> Patric III earl of Dunbar by attorney, appears *versus* Roger de Merlay in a plea to do him the customary and right services demanded from him for his freehold held of the Earl in Wytton, Stanton, Wyndegates, Horsley, Ritton, and Leveriche.[148]

The contestants of course knew exactly what these "customary and right services" were. We don't, but we can make comparisons with the sort of services rendered to the king at around the same time. From the time of King William I, rents for land had been paid in the form of food, and this went on until the reign of Henry I, the time we are considering. There is a reliable witness who described the process which was troublesome, and not popular with the tenants. Richard Fitz Nigel was the treasurer of the king's exchequer.

> I myself have met certain persons who remember seeing provisions carried to court at stated times from royal manors ... As time passed ... a host of farmers flocked to the court, lodging complaints, or accosting the king in his travels ... holding up their ploughs ... for they were oppressed by innumerable burdens because they had to transport provisions great distances from their own homes.

Gradually, the ancient food rents were changed to a money payment. For wheat for bread for a hundred men, it became one shilling; for a ram or sheep four pence; for the fodder of twenty horses, four pence.[149]

By 1247, the records show evidence that the services at Beanley itself had been changed "from a drengage into a service payment of 12 marks of silver annually".[150] This would almost certainly have happened between the Merlay and Gospatric heirs too.

It looks like de Merlays at the time of Juliana's marriage would have had the great inconvenience of delivering food rents to the family of the original native earls, by horse and cart, from lands near Morpeth over the hills to a collection point in the *serjeanty* of Beanley.

Thus although Juliana's dowry brought prestige to the de Merlays, there was more to it than a mere girl bringing wealth to her new family. She and her family retained rights over these lands, which remained in the *serjeanty* of Beanley under her father's control. This would considerably enhance her own personal feeling of self-worth. She may well have had a say in how the lands of her dowry were to be used, with later significance when she and her husband established Newminster Abbey.

---

[147] Hodgson, p 8
[148] Calendar of Documents relating to Scotland, i, p 462, no 2342; also p 319, no 1719; 320 no 1728
[149] Dialogue of the Exchequer, English Historical Documents, pp 515- 516
[150] Calendar of Documents relating to Scotland, i, p 316 – 317, no 1711

Did Juliana meet King Henry I of England?

The words of King Henry seem very personal in the marriage charter. "Notice, all of you, that I have given Juliana in free marriage to Ranulph de Merlay." It produces an image of the king sitting around a table with his quill pen in hand, his seal ready to be affixed, all the witnesses ready at hand, and Gospatric family members nearby. It would be pleasing to picture the young Juliana shyly gazing at the most important man in the foreign kingdom of England, the man whose permission her father needed so that she could be married.

Because I would really have liked to find evidence of such a meeting, I tried very hard to track down King Henry's movements in the north of England or Scotland in the first decade or so of his reign. The document, the *Regesta Regum Anglo-Normannorum, 1066 – 1154,* is an impressive chronological assemblage of the charters signed by Henry I.[151] The document contains definite evidence that the king was in the north in 1105, around the time when it seems logical to me that Henry would have agreed the lands and marriage charters with Gospatric II.

There are seven charters for that year. Two are from Pontefract, three from York, one from Nottingham, and one from Barton on the Humber. They are of considerable interest in themselves. In Pontefract, he signed an order that the monks of Selby should have their fish-stew as granted by William I.[152] In Barton, he addressed Liulf and Aluric of Corbridge, and all the barons and faithful of Northumberland, that no-one was to hunt in the forests of Ranulf Bishop of Durham, either in Northumberland or Durham. Guy de Balliol was specially forbidden. Anyone found doing so should make amends as if he had hunted in the New Forest.[153]

It seems certain that the gossip would have spread as far as the de Merlays of Morpeth about Guy de Balliol's bad ways.

The version of Juliana's marriage charter with which we are familiar, however, appears to be of a later date. A summary of it appears in the *Regesta Regum Anglo-Normannorum*.[154] It was signed "at Woodstock", as can be seen in our version above, where Henry I signed charters in 1123, 1127, 1130 and 1132. Two of the witnesses, William Maldut and William of Pont del Harche (more properly spelled as William of Pont de l'Arche) had been chamberlains to King Henry I in this period.[155] The version which we've looked at carefully above was thus probably a confirmation charter of an earlier one which has not survived.[156] As we can be fairly certain that Juliana and Ranulph's son William was old enough to sign a charter in 1129, we know that the marriage must have been earlier than 1123. Support for this interpretation can be found in the historian Greenwell's account of the Gospatrics in his statement: "This marriage cannot have taken place much later than 1100."[157] He specifies 1100 because it was the year when Henry I came to the throne.

Thus, how and where Juliana's original marriage charter was compiled we will never know, and it is rather disappointing that we can't picture Juliana being present as the king's seal was affixed to the charters which concerned her.

---

[151] Regesta Regum Anglo-Normannorum, Vol 2, 1066 – 1154, Charles Johnson and H Cronne, Oxford, Clarendon, 1956
[152] As above, p 45, no 711
[153] As above, p 45
[154] As above, p 278, no 1848. For the dates at Woodstock, see pp xxx and xxxi
[155] As above, p xiv
[156] Support for this interpretation can be found in Greenwell, p 181, and in Hamilton, p 38 and 261
[157] Greenwell, p 181

Edgar's puzzling charter

Juliana's brother Edgar had a reputation as being a bit of a wild character.[158] Immediately after the appearance of her marriage charter in the rolls both in Hodgson's manuscript and in the Newminster Cartulary is a confirmation charter by Edgar.[159] Why should a brother's confirmation be needed after the words of the king?

> And Edgar the son of count Cospatric confirmed this [the king's] charter, as follows in these words.

> Edgarus Gospatricii son of the count to all his friends, French and English, greetings. You should know that **I have given** and granted to Juliana my sister that land which my and her father, namely Count Gospatric, gave and granted to her in free marriage, namely: Witton, Horsley, Stanton, Ritton, Wyndegates, and Leuerchilde …

It is worth noting here that Edgar appears to have some rights over these lands as he states that he himself has given and granted them to his sister. And then, this.

> They are to be held by her and her heirs **from me and my heirs.** [The holdings are] in lands, waters, all forests belonging to those lands and in mills, ponds, meadows, pastures, paths and outside paths, with all things belonging to those lands. Three services are excepted, namely common military service in the earldom, cornage, and common work at the castle in the earldom. And I wish that she should hold the aforesaid lands as freely and quit of services just as my father gave them to her in free marriage. Farewell.[160]

Here, we read in the phrase "from me and my heirs" that he himself had held these lands, before his sister. That is unexpected. Had the townships originally, or in some way since the lands charter, been passed to him by his father?

Another point to note is the list of witnesses. Those in the first charter of the king are names with which most of us would not be familiar, like John Peuerell de Baelcamp, William Maldut and similar. The witnesses to Edgar's however are very different. They include these men from local places.

> Johanne deacon of Bewick
> Willelmo priest of Stanton
> Ostredo priest of Hartburn
> Grimbauldo de Merlay
> Cospatric son of Leuenoc
> Cospatric of Horsley and Alexander his son
> Aschetil of Stanton
> Godfrid of Wingate.[161]

Horsley, which would be our modern Longhorsley, Wingates, Stanton and Hartburn are all near Morpeth, between the rivers Wansbeck and the Coquet. These witnesses are from the townships of Juliana's dowry. Why should Edgar's witnesses be so different from the king's?

His charter also contains more detail about the conditions, confirming to his sister all the ordinary rights and everything belonging to the townships, in waters, forests, woods, mills, mill-ponds, meadows, pastures and roads.

I can't help wondering if some pressure was being placed on Edgar.

The de Merlays might have wanted it, in the same way as they wanted the king's charter, to prove the rights of their new daughter-in-law to these lands. Juliana herself might have wanted it if she suspected Edgar would try to grasp the lands from her. Perhaps the witnesses were

---

[158] Richard Prior of Hexham, pp 51 – 52; Elsa Hamilton, p 39
[159] The full transcription from the Surtees Society volume can be seen as Appendix 3
[160] Translation by Gail Boyes. Guidance on interpretation from Teresa Saunders. And see Greenwell, p 36
[161] Newminster Cartulary p 269. See Appendix 3 for the full Latin version.

assembled by the de Merlay family so that everyone was clear that the lands were Juliana's and not her brother's.

Another point to consider is that the lands are to be inherited by "her heirs". Her husband's name is not mentioned. Once again, this is a hint that the Gospatric family were holding back some influence.

We might look too at the names of the witnesses. Three are Gospatrics, and they may well have been from the wider family. This idea reinforces Elsa Hamilton's earlier suggestion that perhaps there never was a complete exile of the Gospatric family, and that when he left Northumberland in 1072, Gospatric I had seen it as a temporary arrangement. Perhaps Juliana was not going into a land of total strangers.

A move back into the ancient earldom
Gospatric II was looking out for his family indeed. As well as Juliana's dowry of the lands closer to Morpeth, he arranged that her brothers gained townships in the north of the county.

Edward obtained Edlingham, Hedgley, Lemington, Wutona, Brandon, Branton and Harehope.[162] These were parts of the previous lands of Uncle Edmund and Winnoc the hunter.

Edgar obtained the former lands of Morel, the townships of Bewick and Eglingham.[163] Later, Edgar married the heiress Aliz, whose inheritance made him a large and established landowner at Caistron in the upper Coquet valley.

Juliana's own dowry was largely from the lands of Liulf.

Most of these acquisitions are not dated, so it is not easy to know whether her brothers were actively in ownership of these lands when Juliana came to Morpeth, or if it happened after she was settled. However, it seems likely that, during the years of her married life, there would have been connections and visiting.

Thus the lands granted to Gospatric II and to Juliana as her dowry may have been something of a restoration, a recovery. Her father may have seen the transfers of land, taking place only thirty or forty years after the exile of Gospatric I, as a move back into the ancient earldom.

As for William de Merlay, in his new barony at Morpeth, this acquisition of land to the north of his barony would increase his local influence. And might he already have been thinking, as had Robert de Mowbray at Tynemouth, about a new and prestigious church or abbey near Morpeth, and how hard-working monks would help to develop the battered lands of his barony?

Much was centred upon this girl. Her dowry would support her husband's family and bring back some influence to the Gospatrics; an arrangement between her father, her father-in-law and the king of England would control an important north/south route; there was even the possibility of a new abbey. Juliana was an important young lady.

---

[162] Greenwell, p 56;
[163] As above, pp 32-33

Sibilla and Juliana, mother and daughter

Juliana and her mother Sibilla would have been paying close attention during the course of all these negotiations. How they felt about it all is not recorded. Their presence was taken for granted, and although we cannot know for certain, their acquiescence assumed.

There is one ascertainable fact, and one only, that we have about Juliana's mother Sibilla. It is her appearance in the *Liber Vitae* of Durham Cathedral.[164] This document is mainly a list of thousands of names, started in the ninth century at Lindisfarne and continued in the Norman period.

The original Liber Vitae is in the British Library, but we can look a Surtees Society volume, available in local libraries.[165] There we will find what we need.

> Edwardus filius comitis Cospat'c
> Waldeuus filius ejus
> Sibilla mater ejus
> Johannes filius Waldeui
> Auiza uxor W.
>
> Edward son of count Cospatric
> Waldeve his son
> Sibilla his mother
> John son of Waldeve
> Auiza wife of Waldeve.[166]

There she is. Our own Juliana's mother. Edward was one of Sibilla's sons and Juliana's brother. By the time of this entry, Sibilla was the great-grandmother of John, the youngest person on the list, and Juliana was his great-aunt.

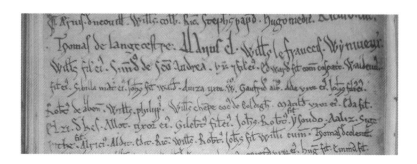

Look at the fourth line down. The second word is Sibilla

From Liber Vitae collotype, Surtees Soc 1923, folio 60

We do not know what was the reason for this four-generation entry in the *Liber Vitae*, and it is all the evidence we have for the name and elusive existence of Juliana's mother. The family tree produced by historian Rev Greenwell uses the *Liber Vitae* for the single source of Sibilla's name.

As all we know is her name, we can do no more than consider how she would have felt once her only daughter was to leave home, and how seldom she might see her again. We have considered that there may have been family members not too far from Morpeth, which might ease some of her anxiety. As for Juliana, she would have been excited, but also uncertain and anxious, knowing that she would be moving into a strange family of whose language she knew little. But both the mother and daughter would have understood Juliana's role, as the historian Lisa Bitel explains.

---

[164] Rev William Greenwell, The House of Gospatric, Northumberland County History Vol VII, p 104
[165] Liber Vitae, Vol 1, Surtees Society 1923, folio 60
[166] Liber Vitae, Surtees Society Vol 13, 1841, p 102

A woman's best hope was marriage, whereby she might start a household with the combined capital of her dowry and her mate's inheritance. She could also complete what was, from her family's perspective, an important job of linking them to another family, acting as ambassador to the new group into which she married – and most women did, indeed, get married. Theirs too was the crucial task of reproduction. … If they refused matches, fought with their in-laws, or bore no children, the family died out.[167]

And so it happened. The mother accepted it, and the daughter knew she must move, and that her role was to produce sons. But she was taking her dignity with her in the form of her dowry and the pride of her descent from kings and queens and earls. The time when Gospatric I had resisted the conquerors was past, and a new generation was taking over. Everything was set in place for the marriage and Juliana's new life with Ranulph de Merlay in Morpeth.

Sources for Juliana's marriage charter

Hodgson's History of Morpeth, p 107
Hodgson writing in 1832 transcribed a manuscript which he had seen held by a William Lawson of Longhirst, which was in the handwriting of the time of Queen Elizabeth or earlier. It had then come into the possession of Lord William Howard, who after a dispute with Francis Dacre inherited the barony of Morpeth. On the back of this manuscript, Hodgson tells us, the following memorandum had been written by William Howard.

> COLLECTIONS touching the Merlaies lands in com. Northumbriae, found among Mr Francis Dacre's paps, and delivered by Mr Bullen. 1616. WH

Hodgson explains that the Latin in the manuscript was "exceedingly incorrect", and that he had tried with partial success to correct it. He transcribed the marriage charter in full, followed by Edgar's confirmation which includes the phrase "from me and my heirs".

The "ancient roll" in the appendix to the Newminster Cartulary, p 268
Rev John Fowler in 1878 wrote that the roll is "unfortunately incomplete at both ends. In its present state it consists of seven skins sewn together, and is 12 ft. 2in. long by 10½ in broad. The first skin is much decayed."

Juliana's marriage charter however is reproduced in full, followed by her brother Edgar's, and it also includes the phrase "from me and my heirs".

Dugdale's Baronage of England, vol 2, p 570
In this classic work of 1675, Dugdale describes Juliana's marriage arrangement, and gives as his source "Ex coll.R.Gl.S". This means *From the collection of Robert Glover, Somerset Herald.* Glover was a royal herald between 1544 and 1588. He collected and copied most of the English medieval rolls of arms. His collection was not printed until 1608, after which it was seen and praised by Dugdale. This would be another original and reliable source of Juliana's marriage to Ranulph, and perhaps one of the earliest.

Dugdale's Monasticon Anglicanum,
In the version of 1717, **vol 2, p 800,** taken from the section referring to Newminster Abbey, the charters of both King Henry and Edgar, are summarised.

In the 1846 version, Vol 5, page 399, both charters are written out, but do not contain the words "from me and my heirs".

The "spurious" charter
There is another "spurious" or unreliable charter confirming Juliana's marriage, which leads us down a dead end. Curious readers may consult Appendix 4.

---

[167] Lisa Bitel, Women in Early Medieval Europe, Cambridge, 2002, p 164

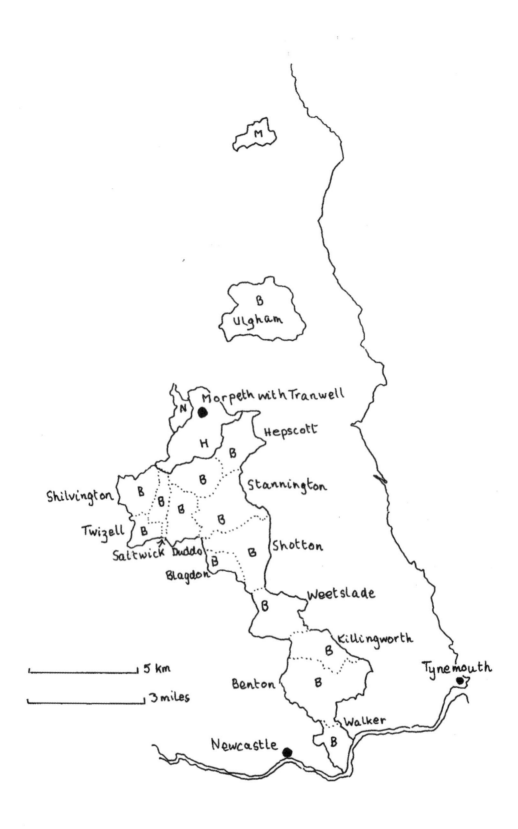

M

B
Ulgham

N ● Morpeth with Tranwell
Hepscott
H
B
B
Shilvington B
Stannington
B B
B
Twizell B
Shotton
Saltwick Duddo B
Blagdon B
Weetslade
B
Killingworth
B
Benton B
Tynemouth ●
Walker
Newcastle ● B

5 km
3 miles

*Lands in the likely control of the de Merlay
barony in about 1113*

Ranulph's offer to Juliana

Lands for a bride

Juliana was a prize. She was no humbled, conquered native, but the daughter of one of the king of Scotland's most powerful nobles, Gospatric II of Dunbar. To win her, and bring her to Morpeth, Ranulph had to make a tempting offer. What could Ranulph offer his bride?

Certainly, if she married him, he would make her the wife of a future baron of Morpeth, and the mistress of some lands which were part of her lost ancestral heritage.

But which lands? Here is a map of the barony of Morpeth at the time of Ranulph's proposal of marriage, around the year 1113.

This map is the result of quite a lot of detective work. Let me take you through the process, and you can decide if my reasoning is convincing.

If we think back as far as we can, we have worked out in the previous chapters that, probably in the 1080s and almost certainly by 1095, William de Merlay had built his castle at Morpeth under the patronage of Earl Robert de Mowbray. Ranulph and Juliana's marriage would have taken place about two decades after 1095, not a very long time after the fall of de Mowbray. William de Merlay controlled certain lands around Morpeth at that time which would later pass to his son.

You will see from the map that there are several pockets. The named townships are based on the 1860s Ordnance Survey maps, as in previous chapters.

The home demesne – marked H

First of all, there must have been land immediately around the castle at Ha' Hill under the baron's close control. This was the *demesne* land, the home land, which the baron would keep for the direct provision of himself and his family. It was probably not sub-infeudated, or sub-let, to any tenants. Morpeth itself included Catchburn, Stobhill and Park House, and Tranwell and High Church. It seems logical that this area would belong to the castle.

Around Newminster Abbey – marked N

Some of the earliest knowledge we have of the Morpeth barony comes from Ranulph and Juliana's foundation of Newminster Abbey in 1138. The foundation charter to the abbey includes lands between Morpeth and Mitford, and describes an area from Fulbeck to the Cottingburn to the Wansbeck.

> All the valley between Morpeth and Hebron, as the rivulet, which is called Fulbeck, runs and falls into Cottingburn, and as Cottingburn runs … as far as the Wansbeck, and thus up to the boundary between me and William Bertram.[168]

As Ranulph had rights over this land that he could donate later to the abbey, this must have been part of the original barony.

These two sets of townships, marked H and N, were the inner demesne, the home farms.

Wansbeck to Tyne – marked B

But the barony was much greater than this, and we can work out its full extent from the *knights' fees,* areas of land held by the William de Merlay's knights.

---

[168] Translation by Hodgson, Morpeth, p 45

Like all the Norman barons, he was required to provide the king with the services of knights, in his case four. These knights could be called up by the king whenever he wanted for his wars. Military service was later usually converted to a payment of money, but at first the knights' fees were based on land.

Hodgson summarised the knights' fees on page 7 of his *History of Morpeth,* in three stages.

Firstly, the earliest record of the four fees was recorded in 1165, and Hodgson gives as his source Lib. Nig. 339. You would probably yawn and go to sleep if I told you how hard it was to find Lib. Nig. 339. However, I did. Here it is.[169]

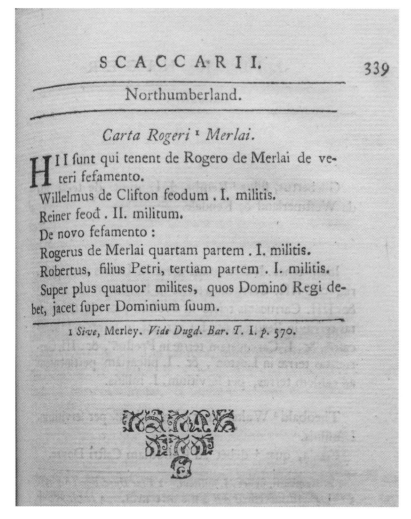

With thanks to the Society of Antiquaries of Newcastle upon Tyne

Photo by Denis Peel

In 1165, King Henry II required all his barons to inform him if they were providing the full service of knights' fees to which he was due. I eventually learned that Lib Nig is a shortened form of *Liber Niger Scaccarii*, which means *Black Book of the Exchequer*.[170]

By 1165, Juliana and Ranulph's son Roger was baron of Morpeth. The *veteri fefamento* or old fees dated back to the time of Henry I, William of Clifton holding one fee and Reiner two. By the time of Henry II, of the *novo fefamento,* or new fees, Roger de Merlay himself owed one quarter of a fee, and Robert the son of Peter owed a third part. To make up the full four fees, Roger provided what was owing from his own demesne.

---

[169] Photo by Denis Peel
[170] Liber Niger Scaccarii, ed T Hearne, 1771, p 339; also see Cartae Baronum, in English Historical Documents, pp 903 - 906

For the purposes of our map, we learn only that the township of Clifton near Morpeth was part of the barony.

Secondly, Hodgson reported that in 1219, Juliana's and Ranulph's grandson, Roger de Merlay II, confirmed that he held the barony of Morpeth by the service of four knights.[171] This record does not name the townships.

Thirdly, Hodgson gives a full list of townships in about the year 1240, in the time of Roger de Merlay III. In other parts of Hodgson's histories, he gives as his source the Testa de Neville. The townships are also carefully listed in the Book of Fees and in the Newminster Cartulary. Here they are.

      Morpeth with Tranwell
      Ulgham
      Hepscott
      Shilvington
      Twizell
      Saltwick
      Duddo East
      Duddo West
      Clifton
      Caldwell
      Stannington
      Shotton
      Blagdon
      Weetslade North
      Weetslade South
      Killingworth
      Benton
      Walker.

The tenants are also named.

      Ranulph de Merlay held Hepscott by one quarter of a new knight's fee
      Hugh de Gubium held Shilvington by half a new knight's fee
      Richard de Dudden held Dudden West by half a new knight's fee
      William Conyers held Clifton and Caldwell by one old knight's fee
      John de Plessys held Shotton, with Plessey, Blagdon and North Weetslade by one old knight's fee
      Galfrid de Weetslade held South Weetslade by one third of an old knight's fee
      Adam Baret held Walker by half an old fee
      Robert de Cambow held one carucate in Saltwick by one tenth of a new knight's fee.[172]

Adding up the total of tenancies, we arrive at just over four fees at the time of Henry III when Roger de Merlay III was the baron of Morpeth. The same four fees go back to 1219 and 1166, taking us back to the time of Henry I. We may thus reasonably assume that these knights' fees were part of William de Merlay's earliest barony.

By placing these named townships side by side on the map, we can see that the de Merlay barony stretched continuously from the Wansbeck to the Tyne, with an outlier at Ulgham. There must have been important decisions made in the earliest days when Earl Robert de Mowbray and William de Merlay established the barony. If he had land as far as the Tyne, William would have been able to keep in close contact with Earl Robert's fortifications at Tynemouth and Newcastle. With a harbour on the river, he would have access to his place of origin in Normandy. He would be able to import delicious French wine, otherwise unavailable in chilly Northumberland, and export his own produce.

---

[171] Hodgson, Morpeth, p 7; also Hodgson's History of Northumberland, Part III Vol I, p 232-233, from the Testa de Neville 1219
[172] Hodgson, Morpeth, pp 7–8; also Part III Vol I, p 208. Book of Fees, HMSO, 1923, p 1117; Hodgson, Morpeth, p 8; Hodgson History of Northumberland Part III, Vol i, p 208; Newminster Cartulary p 267-268, with a few slight differences from Hodgson

Importantly, he had a continuous strip of fertile agricultural land from Morpeth to the Tyne, with routes under his control. This was a worthwhile reward for his services in the conquest. And it was a tempting offer to Juliana's father in the marriage negotiations.

The long line of townships from the Tyne north almost to Morpeth takes us as far as Hepscott and Clifton. The three townships around Morpeth, together with the one donated in 1138 to Newminster Abbey, complete the continuous range of the barony from the Tyne to the castle.

Ulgham: the eagle's nest – marked B

Ulgham was a separate area three or so miles to the north east. In the 1138 foundation charter to Newminster, Ranulph de Merlay had given land there to the monks.

> … at Ulgham, I have given to them to build their granges upon, from the Eagle's nest to the well of Erard, and as the stream of that well runs into the Lima …[173]

Perhaps the de Merlays controlled more land between Morpeth and Ulgham, but there is no surviving evidence of this.

A castle at Warkworth? – marked M

There is another outlying township quite a long way north. This is Morwick, near Warkworth. In the title page to his *History of Morpeth*, Hodgson presented this surprising quotation from Leland.

> Morley of Morpeth, was ons Lord of Wercwoth castel on l'Coket Mouth.[174]

Did Warkworth Castle once belong to de Merlay? Warkworth castle, that great stone structure on the coastal route through Northumberland? Could this have been part of the Merlay estates that Ranulph would offer to Juliana?

Hodgson seemed to think so.

> The source of the quotation from Leland seems to be strengthened by William de Merlay's first grant of Morwick, in the parish of Warkworth, to the monks of Durham.[175]

There was of course no great stone castle at Warkworth in those days. We have already seen that William de Merlay had granted land at Morwick, near Warkworth, to the monks of Durham. This means that he was in control of land there around the time of the marriage of his son to Juliana, and that is why it is on our map. He may have held other land between Morpeth and Warkworth, although we cannot know this.

Those five areas together give us a good idea of size of the Morpeth barony at or around 1113. It was not the greatest barony in Northumberland by any means. It was much smaller than that of the Vescy barony at Alnwick which owed 12 knights' fees, but comparable with the next largest of the Baliols of Bywell who had five, the Bertrams of Mitford and the Bolbecs of Styford who both also had five, and the Muschamps of Wooler who had four. Most of the remaining baronies were much less formidable.[176]

Thus, the barony of Morpeth was worthy. There may have been other unrecorded pockets of land, too, as we have observed. Further work around the boundaries of the neighbouring baronial families, in particular of the Bertrams of Mitford and Bothal, would without doubt enlighten us, but that must wait for another time.

I've enjoyed working all this out, and you the reader may judge whether or not these boundaries seem convincing. This is the land, I suggest, which Ranulph would have been able to offer his

---

[173] Hodgson, Morpeth, p 45
[174] Hodgson, Morpeth, title page
[175] As above, p 4
[176] C H Hunter Blair, Baronys and Knights of Northumberland, Archaeologia Aeliana, 4th Series, 1952, p 16

new wife in or around the year 1113. It would have impressed Gospatric II, Juliana's father, and her dowry would have impressed the de Merlays. The arrangement suited everyone, including the king.

Morpeth was part of King Henry's plan

The marriage of Juliana and Ranulph was all part of King Henry's plan. He needed to establish order after the devastation of the conquest years and all that had gone before them. The castle on the Wansbeck, and the alliance of Ranulph's and Juliana's families through their marriage, were among the earliest changes he was making.

When he became king in 1100, the Norman conquest had hardly progressed northwards since the death of King William I in 1087. There were royal castles at Newcastle, Tynemouth and Bamburgh, controlled by sheriffs since Earl Robert de Mowbray's downfall, but the countryside was almost unoccupied by the conquerors.[177] The new king began a programme of placing his men, often called his "new men", in strategic situations throughout the county along the river valleys, and protecting the fertile eastern plain. The historian Kapelle makes a clear point that the king considered the former earldom of Northumberland as his own to dispense with as he wished.

> The Northumbrian countryside was apparently considered royal demesne. This was, of course, a legal fiction typical of Norman justice, but it was useful to Henry, who filled the Far North with his supporters ... Above the Tyne he created a line of baronies running to the Tweed.

> In the Tyne valley and the hills to the north, Walter de Bolbec ... received Styford, and in the same region Robert de Umfraville obtained Prudhoe, which was probably augmented before 1135 by the grant of the serjeanty of Redesdale.

> To the east and the north, Henry apparently gave Mitford to William Bertram or his father, and perhaps the neighbouring lordship of Bothal to a son of William. Mitford, Bothal and Morpeth, which may have been an older lordship, dominated the lowlands of Northumberland from the Tyne to the Coquet.

> Beyond them six new baronies were created. Morwick and Hadston adjoined the royal demesne of Warkworth ... North of these fees were Alnwick, the greatest of all the baronies, for Eustace fitz John, and Ellingham for Nicholas de Grenville. Finally, Robert de Muschamp was given Wooler in the Till valley, and Walter Espec received Wark on the Tweed.[178]

The map which follows shows the baronies which controlled the river routes into the county as described by Kapelle. We can see Morpeth castle's position in the overall pattern.

---

[177] Kapelle, p 195-199
[178] Kapelle, p 199

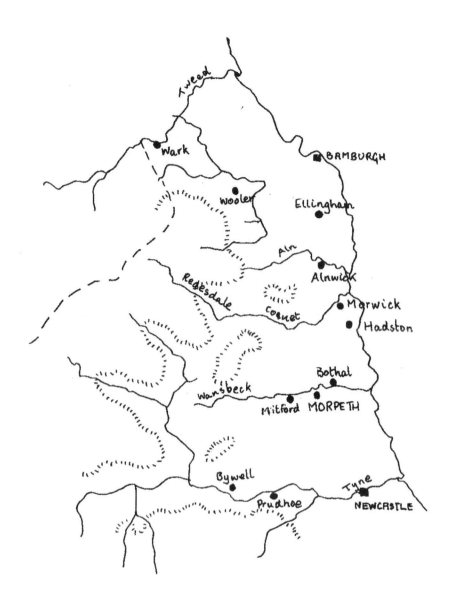

Morpeth's place among Northumberland's castles protecting the coastal plain.

Juliana's sons and the ancestral land

The barony of Morpeth would play its part in King Henry's plan for control of the Northumberland borderlands. Ranulph was the heir to a substantial landholding, and this he could offer his bride.

As his wife, Juliana would share some of her family's ancestral territory, and if she had sons it would pass to them. The name Gospatric might be lost, but her bloodline, her genetic inheritance, would continue. Her father accepted Ranulph's father's offer. Juliana would play her part in the Gospatric family story. She would come to Morpeth.

The names Sibilla and Juliana

The names Sibilla and Juliana are more Greek or Latin than English, hinting at the widespread cultural links of the Gospatric family.

Sibilla is found in various spellings. The name comes originally from the sibyls, women with special powers of prophecy and intercession with the gods of ancient Greece.

The name was in fashion in the period we are considering.

Sybilla of Conversano was the duchess of Normandy, wife of Duke Robert who built the castle at Newcastle in 1080. She died in 1103, six months after the birth of her son.

Another Sibilla was the wife of King Alexander of Scotland, who came to the throne in 1107. She was the illegitimate daughter of Henry I of England, but this was an advantage rather than an obstacle to her marrying a king.

As wife of Gospatric II, Sibilla's name was clearly still in fashion. Although they chose mainly Anglian names for their sons, they chose a Latin name for their daughter.

Juliana was a martyr and a saint in the Roman Empire of the fourth century. The story appears in the *martyrology* compiled by the Northumbrian monk historian, the Venerable Bede, in the eighth century. She was the daughter of a pagan named Africanus, and as a child was betrothed to the senator Eleusius, an advisor to the Roman emperor. Juliana secretly became a Christian, and refused to marry Eleusius. In the end, her would-be husband had her tortured, and she was eventually beheaded in 304 AD. She became the patron saint of sickness, and was widely venerated in the medieval period.

As a Christian girl, it is quite probable that Juliana knew the story of the saint after whom she was named. There is an accessible version of Saint Juliana's story in Henrietta Leyser's *Medieval Women,* p 58.

This illustration by artist Peter Scholefield shows a timber castle at Hen Domen in Wales, as it might have been around the time when Juliana came to Morpeth.

In our case, we don't know the exact location of the main residence of the de Merlay family, but what we can see from this picture is the sophistication of timber castles at this time.

Morpeth's Romeo and Juliet

Juliana comes to Morpeth

Juliana, granddaughter of the exiled former earl Gospatric of Northumberland, and Ranulph de Merlay, son of a warrior of the Norman Conquest, were to be married.

She was a tender, inexperienced girl of perhaps fifteen years of age, travelling southwards to a new life. She was leaving behind her home in Scotland, her mother and her brothers and sisters, and everything that she had known. Ahead of her lay a new life with a man she knew little about, and whose language she did not speak. Her girlish fears and hopes can only be imagined.

She was an important link in the political schemes of her father and the king of England. Her youthful person was of value, her own dreams barely a consideration. Her role was to produce sons, and by that she would be measured.

Her new home in the timber castle by the Wansbeck awaited her. Her husband's parents, William and Menialda, were ready to welcome her. His brothers Goffrid and Morel and his sister Eustorcia were all waiting to meet her. She knew their names, but nothing of their characters or if they would be kind to her.

And what about her new home? How would she live? All these thoughts would have gone through her mind, over and over again, as she made her way southward.

Marriage

After King Henry and Juliana's father Gospatric II had agreed to the marriage, perhaps there had been a betrothal ceremony something like this described by historian Lisa Bitel.

> The betrothal, or wedding, or both were normally celebrated by the entire community and marked with ceremony – maybe a great banquet with copious drinking, singing, dancing, and plenty of obscene jokes to enhance the fertility of the union. The couple may have signified their union with symbolic gifts, possibly a ring. They may also have exchanged a kiss on the mouth, which was a medieval symbol for all sorts of unions – the same kiss united a lord and his vassal. Thus were man and woman formally joined, even without the benefit of religious ceremony … Often enough, two young people joined by their families began living together immediately without a formal wedding.[179]

We do not know where the marriage was celebrated, whether it was at Juliana's home in Dunbar or in Morpeth. Neither do we know if the couple liked each other. Love was not the main consideration in a dynastic alliance of this sort.

> When arranging a marriage, one thing fathers, mothers, kinsmen, women, the church and lawmakers rarely took official notice of was love. In medieval eyes, marriage was not the monogamous meeting of two hearts beating as one, or the fusion of two individual minds promising eternal love. Yet just because their families participated does not mean that men and women eliminated affection from the process … or that their desires were unimportant. We do know that men and women fell in love, sometimes with their spouses, and that others helped them find their soul-mates.[180]

Neither was there necessarily a religious ceremony. Customs varied everywhere, but nine hundred years ago, the formalities were not yet fixed. Around the year 1113, the time we are considering, all that was needed were the statements "I take you as my wife … I take you as my husband". After saying those words, everyone including legal and religious officials accepted the couple as married.[181]

---

[179] Lisa Bitel, Women in Early Medieval Europe, Cambridge, 2002, p 172
[180] As above, p174
[181] Henrietta Leyser, Medieval Women, Phoenix, 1996, p 106

Juliana's first nights with Ranulph, in a secluded space in her castle in Scotland or in the timber castle in Morpeth, will for ever remain her personal secret. Historian Henrietta Leyser has written a chapter in her book, *Medieval Women*, called *Sex, Marriage and Motherhood*. Although the chapter contains quite a lot of information for the later thirteenth and fourteenth century, there is little from as long ago as the period of Juliana's marriage. But there is this one excerpt from this time which describes a cosmetic aid for love.

> Before sexual intercourse, a woman should rub her breast, nipples and genitals with a powder made of dried roses, cloves, nutmeg, galingale and laurel.[182]

We may hope that the young couple did in fact find love together. Their relationship certainly did result in three baby boys, one after another, as the years went on.

A woman's home is her timber castle

Juliana's new home was in the de Merlays' timber castle by the Wansbeck. We have no details about the interior of Morpeth's castle, but we can compare it with a rare description of one in northern France built very close in time to Juliana and Ranulph's marriage. In about 1120, Lord Arnold of Ardres, near Calais, ordered a new castle on the site of an earlier one which had been damaged in a war.

> Arnold built upon the motte at Ardres a timber house which was a marvellous example of the carpenter's craft. The carpenter ... created an almost impenetrable labyrinth, piling storeroom upon storeroom, chamber upon chamber, room upon room, extending the larders and granaries into the cellars, and building the chapel in a convenient place overlooking all else.
>
> He made it of three floors, the topmost storey supported by the second as though suspended in the air.
>
> The first storey was at ground level, and here were the cellars and granaries, the great chests, casks, butts and other domestic utensils.
>
> On the second storey were the residential apartments and common living quarters, and there were the larders, the rooms of the bakers and the butlers, and the great chamber of the lord and his lady, where they slept, on to which adjoined a small room which provided the sleeping quarters of the maidservants and children.
>
> Here in the inner part of the great chamber there was a small private room where at early dawn or in the evening, or in sickness, or for warming the maids and weaned children, they used to light a fire.
>
> On this floor also was the kitchen, which was on two levels. On the lower level pigs were fattened, geese tended, chickens and other fowls killed and prepared. On the upper level the cooks and stewards worked and prepared the delicate dishes for the lords, which entailed much hard work on the part of the cooks, and here also the meals for the household and servants were prepared each day.
>
> On the top floor of the house there were small rooms in which, on one side, the sons of the lord slept when they wished to do so, and, on the other side, his daughters as they were obliged. There too the watchmen, the servants appointed to keep the household, and the ever-ready guards, took their sleep when they could.
>
> There were stairs and corridors from floor to floor, from the residential quarters to the kitchen, from chamber to chamber, and from the main building to the loggia where they used to sit for conversation and recreation, as also from the loggia to the chapel which was like the temple of Solomon in its ceiling and its decoration.[183]

---

[182] As above, p 101
[183] Lambert of Ardres, cited in Robert Higham, pp 115 - 116

The account was written by a priest called Lambert between 1194 and 1203, and was written to flatter Lord Arnold's family. From these details, we may picture a little of Juliana's life.

The ageing William and Menialda would occupy the great chamber. Juliana and Ranulph would occupy one of the small rooms on the top floor of the house. Ranulph's brothers would be nearby, sleeping there when they felt like it presumably between their youthful lordly antics, and Eustorcia, his sister, in a small room where she was obliged to sleep to preserve her maidenly virtues.

As time went on, and Juliana and Ranulph's sons were born, the growing family would take over the greater space used by the old couple.

Certainly the whole establishment seems like a wonderful place for children, with plenty of animals in evidence, servants in the kitchen who might be persuaded to part with tasty bites, and hidey-holes in which to make dens.

What is also clear is that a castle like this was no humble log-cabin abode. It provided for sophisticated class of society, who ate delicious meals prepared by well-organised household servants.

Exactly how similar Morpeth's castle was to the one at Ardres, despite my confident comparisons, we cannot be sure, particularly because we have no information about the location of the bailey, the enclosure surrounding the high motte itself where many of the outbuildings would be found. Nevertheless, as the writers of the book *Timber Castles* make clear, bare green *mottes* in a place like Morpeth cannot give a true impression of a lively structure like that of Ardres, in which the upper floors overlap the one below.

> Although it would be impossible to draw a plan of each floor from the information given, a clear impression emerges of a three-storey tower whose uppermost level was jettied out from the one below. The account is an invaluable corrective to one-dimensional excavated ground plans, even more to the countless bare earthworks about which nothing at all is known.[184]

The illustration at the beginning of this chapter shows us that Juliana was likely to be arriving at a well-designed set of buildings which offered a good level of comfort. This picture is based on the excavation at the motte and bailey castle at Hen Domen, in Wales, as it may have looked after 1086 and before about 1215.[185] The earlier years of this phase include the time when Juliana arrived at Morpeth. In our case, we don't know the exact location of the main residence of the de Merlay family, either within the bailey or on the summit of the dome.

From now on, I will always look at Morpeth's motte at Ha' Hill with new eyes.

Lambert the priest also wrote a pleasing description of Arnold's young wife at Ardres.

> Arnold the Young's wife, Petronilla, was a young woman, pleasing to God, simple and God-fearing, and either she served God with serious application in church, or amongst her maids put her youthful mind to childish jokes and dancing, and similarly to games and dolls. Often in the summer, inspired at least as much by her simple nature as by the agility of her body, she took off her clothes, except for her shift, let herself go and went into the fish pond, not really to wash or bathe, but rather to cool off and stretch herself out.
>
> Here and there in the streams and bends of the water she was swimming, now face down, now on her back or now disappearing into the water, now whiter than snow she showed herself or her white shift dry above the water in full view of the knights, no less than her maids.

---

[184] Higham and Barker, pp 115-116
[185] Hen Domen, Montgomery: a timber castle on the English-Welsh border, Exeter University Press, 2000

Behaving as amicably in these and similar ways and manners, she showed to her husband, to her knights, as well as to her people, how pleasing and just lovable she was.[186]

This is the young Juliana as I like to think of her; playing games with her maids, dancing, playing with dolls, and enjoying the waters of the Wansbeck. Lucky Ranulph indeed, if he had such a pleasing and lovable wife. He would be the envy of his knightly friends. I'm not quite sure though how innocent the priestly descriptions really were.

Childbirth

All we know about Juliana's pregnancy and childbirth was that she and Ranulph had three surviving children, all boys, William, Roger and Osbert. Henrietta Leyser's book tells us about traditional advice given to a young pregnant woman of a higher social group at that time.

> Annotations in manuscripts are an indication that traditional remedies were still in use at least until the thirteenth century. Familiar prognostications are likely to have been handed down: the mother who walks slowly, for example, and has hollow eyes, will bear a son; if she walks quickly and has swollen eyes, the baby will be a girl, if she walks with her weight on her heels – a boy; on her toes – a girl.

and

> A pregnant woman is to be earnestly warned that she should eat nothing salty or sweet, or drink beer, or eat swine's flesh or anything fat, or drink to intoxication, or travel by road, or ride too much on horseback, lest the child be born before the proper time.

> Nor is she to eat 'bull's flesh or ram's or buck's or boar's or gander's or that of any animal that can beget' or the child may be hump-backed.[187]

Can we imagine that Juliana would walk slowly, with hollow eyes, while pregnant with her sons? She may well have been a sprightly and lively young woman. Even so, as the birth times of her babies arrived, she must have had anxious moments. Death in childbirth was common. As Juliana gave birth successfully to three sons, we know that she was a lucky survivor or we wouldn't have had this story.

The couple may have had other children as one in five died before the age of five, Leyser tells us.[188] That we will never know. But Juliana would bring up three boys, and that was one mark of her success as a wife.

Up to her elbows in flour

From her mother-in-law Menialda, Juliana would learn to manage the complex household at their castle.

> Noblewomen managed larger households than did poor women, though performing many similar labors. Women of all stations made bread for their families. Wives and maids, children and nuns, all labored at the same jobs day after day, year after year, generation after generation, to keep house, keep family, keep prosperous, keep the community together.[189]

We can imagine Juliana up to her elbows in flour as she pounded the dough. She would also have probably have been skilled in the arts of spinning, weaving and sewing.

> Every early medieval queen could produce fine needlework and some were justly famous for it. Edith, wife of Edward the Confessor, dressed him in her own handiwork and was an expert spinner … Women won respect for what everyone perceived as their inherent talents, whether applied to the family's shirts or the fine embroidery of ladies' bonnets.[190]

---

[186] Patricia Skinner and Elisabeth van Houts, Medieval Writings on Secular Women, Penguin, 2011, p 159
[187] Leyser, p 124, citing Bald's Leechbook of Medicine
[188] Leyser, pp 122 - 141
[189] Bitel, pp 205-207
[190] Bitel, p 221

As women of a noble family, it is highly likely that Juliana, Menialda and their female attendants were skilled needlewomen.

Who told Gaimar?
What other interests might Juliana have had? Did she enjoy the arts, or the romantic literature which was becoming fashionable? In Morpeth's provincial remoteness, perhaps it is unlikely. We do not have any evidence one way or the other, but there is one intriguing hint.

We have met the evidence of the Anglo-Norman poet Gaimar who provided the first documented mention of Morpeth and the Merlay castle by the Wansbeck in his account of the rebellion of Earl Robert de Mowbray in 1095. No other chronicler mentioned Morpeth and the castle by the Wansbeck, so where did Gaimar get his information? Someone must have told him. Did this have anything to do with Juliana and Ranulph?

Leyser tells us that a fashion for French literature was set by the court of Henry I and his queen Matilda.[191] This fashion was followed in the provinces, and with the encouragement of Constance FitzGilbert in Lincolnshire, Gaimar wrote his *L'estoire des Engleis* probably between 1136 and 1137. This was during the time of Juliana's and Ranulph's married life together. Among the circles of the Norman nobility, which families knew each other? Who visited whom?

Who told Gaimar?

Were the FitzGilberts of Lincolnshire acquainted with Juliana and Ranulph de Merlay? Who might have visited Morpeth along the accessible route between the Scottish and the English courts? Perhaps Juliana or Ranulph told Gaimar, or someone among their acquaintances did. During the chat over the banqueting tables, isn't that what we all talk about? Each other's affairs. Our personal bravery. Family anecdotes.

The ordinary people of Morpeth
We know that there would have been an extensive household of servants in the de Merlay castle. Some would be French speaking associates of the family, but others would be local people who would learn just enough French to do their work. Who would they have been, and what were their jobs?

There is a fascinating document about the householders of King Henry I which names the servants and their payments. Of course minor barons like the de Merlays would have far fewer servants, but the aspirations for the high lifestyle would be similar. The king had a chancellor who was the master of his writing office, and in charge of the seals of his documents. There was the chaplain in charge of the chapel and the relics; the steward who looked after domestic affairs; the dispenser who supervised giving out of bread and other produce; the waferer in charge of producing confectionery; cooks; the keeper of the dishes; the usher of the turnspit; carters who brought in the food; watchmen; the stoker of the fire. All the important officers had their servants, and they were paid in food, wine, candles and money. The servants who used horses as part of their work received a payment for each animal.

The hunting team was equally elaborate. There were horn-blowers, keepers of greyhounds, bloodhounds, running hounds, staghounds; there were huntsmen in charge of the wolf-hunt and the stag-hunt. As hunting parties ranged far and wide, there was a keeper of the tents and a carrier of the bows.[192]

Some of those activities would have taken place at the de Merlay castle. The kitchen would have been bustling, with the comings and goings of horses and carts bringing in produce, the preparation of the bread and the meat, turnspit rotating and the fire being stoked. And how many packs of dogs there were we can only wonder. Wolfhounds? Greyhounds? Bloodhounds?

[191] Leyser, pp 244-145
[192] English Historical Documents, The Establishment of the King's Household, p 422

Staghounds? Imagine them ranging over the hills and woodlands in the valleys of Wansbeck and Font, with the horn-blower leading the way, while the women and children stayed at home waiting to see what the knight-huntsmen brought in.

But as well as those employed in the castle, many others worked in the fields ploughing and harrowing and harvesting, both on their own strips of land and on the home demesne lands of the de Merlays.

From her high viewpoint at the castle, Juliana must often have looked down over the peasant families working in the fields beside the river. These people spoke her English language, even though with some differences from her childhood version in Scotland. Some would be her personal servants. These were the ordinary people of that time, the ancestors of most of us, people like you and me.

One of my favourite anecdotes is a remark by a Morpeth woman after I'd written *The Curious Yards and Alleyways of Morpeth.* I was in a shop, and she was telling me she'd read the book. A friend of hers was asking her what was all this about Ha' Hill. And she said: "I know all about that. That's where they looked down at us from!"

And that is a very good expression of how the local people would have felt. They would see the foreigners up in their castle, looking down at them while they laboured resentfully on the lord's demesne, on land which was no longer their own.

There are no records of how the labouring people felt. Nobody would have thought there was any reason to write about their feelings, but here is a perceptive description from a modern historian.

> In the Anglo-Norman village, the peasant was the typical Englishman, and the affairs of his village furnished him with all the major interest of his life. The fields absorbed his energies in a perpetual struggle with the soil. The manor house embodied his temporal allegiance; in the cottages of his neighbours he found his only social contacts; and to the village church he turned for all that transcended his mundane preoccupations. Outside, all was strange. Fifteen or twenty miles from his cottage door there began an unknown world into which he probably never entered ... The politics of Church and State affected him only indirectly, and he knew little of the wars of princes.
>
> His smaller world was all-demanding, and it was circumscribed. Life in both its natural and supernatural aspects was bounded by familiar landmarks, and its long monotony was punctuated only by the seasons in the surrounding fields ... Harvest and Michaelmas were but as one celebration and the miracle of the spring the inevitable prelude to the Easter Mass. And over all was the unending routine of labour which had continued in its accustomed way unchanged from time without memory, and which must have seemed incapable of change.[193]

The women of the peasant families would have been affected in just the same way as the men of course. The huge impact on their lives of pregnancy, childbirth and bringing up of children in those circumstances goes unmentioned.

This description avoids the devastations of the armies as they passed through, and Northumberland had been particularly unfortunate in this respect. However, in the interludes between the marchings, and in the period of relative calm in the years of Henry I, perhaps this picture does represent life for many of the ordinary people of Morpeth.

Inside the wooden huts
What was life like inside the wooden huts in Morpeth, among the families from whom Juliana would have drawn her servants?

The lowliest villagers lived in hovels, often one-chamber structures made of branches lashed together, and roofed with straw. The floor was of earth, and straw or rushes provided the

---

[193] English Historical Documents, pp 77 - 78

bedding. There was little protection from the elements. Illnesses such as rheumatism and arthritis must have been common. In many cases, animals would share the room, and only in longer houses might there be a wattle-and-daub partition.

In such rooms as these, the women would manage as best they could, helping each other through the dramas of childbirth and rearing of the children. As the communities had so little contact with outsiders, partnering between people with close family relationships must have taken place all the time. This would often produce children with physical and mental disabilities. Many of them would die in childhood, but those who survived would need to depend on charity.

Infant mortality was high. Babies were swaddled in an attempt to avert the common complaint of rickets. When the babies were old enough, and could crawl around in the dirty rushes on the cottage floors, they would put everything they found in their mouth as babies do.

In the winter time, many of the tasks essential to survival would have taken place in the dark and smoky interiors. The men made the wooden platters and spoons, which were the staple domestic equipment, and most of the rough tools needed in cultivations. The women spun and wove the wool from the family sheep, made the poor man's linen from hemp or nettles, and sewing thread also from nettles. They also plaited straw or reeds for neck collars. They peeled rushes, which they then soaked in fat for their rushlights.[194]

Here another description of the work of village women.

> Most women needed no specialized training for labors within or outside of marriage, but only what other women knew and passed on to them as they grew. Peasant girls learned from their mothers and other kinswomen not only clothworking, but the care of chickens and other farmyard animals, milking, cooking, brewing. In the country, they went with their mothers and older female relatives to the fields, learning to weed, harvest and bind sheaves. Older women of their communities – mothers-in-law, aunties, neighbors – also taught the added tasks, which came with maturity, of producing a family and training daughters to join the workforce.[195]

Nowadays we might admire this huge range of skills of the ordinary people which enabled them to sustain life. I certainly do.

Food for the rich: food for the poor

As long as the villagers had enough to eat, their diet was surprisingly nutritious by our modern standards. They had very little access to red meat. Chicken was eaten only occasionally as hens were more valuable for their eggs. Daily food was heavily cereal and vegetable-based. A single pot on the fire would provide soup, to which items were added as they became available. Most of their protein would have been provided by peas and beans, with some fish and bacon.

At the end of winter, stocks of grain would sometimes be used up, and bread would be improvised with ingredients like acorns, beans and peas. Here is a recipe for bread which was still in use in our area in the nineteenth century.

> Bread is made of barley, or barley mixed with grey pease or beans … it is kneaded with water, made into thin unleavened cakes and immediately baked on a girdle. Oatmeal also constitutes a principle article of food with the peasantry, not as bread, but in crowdies or hasty pudding for breakfast; and sometimes for supper, eaten with butter or more commonly with milk.[196]

Wealthier people, like the de Merlay family on Ha' Hill, would have eaten more meat and drunk more alcohol. While Juliana and Ranulph sat down with their family to roasted venison and freshly baked wheaten bread, washed down with imported red wine, the families in the huts were satisfying their hunger with simple girdle-baked bread and a pot of vegetable soup.[197]

---

[194] Olive Tomkeieff, summaries from her Life in Norman England, Batsford, 1966, p 119 and pp 66-67
[195] Bitel, p 207
[196] E Mackenzie, A Historical and Descriptive View of the County of Northumberland, Vol 1,1811, p 231
[197] With thanks to Iona McCleery of Leeds University and Tony Henderson of The Journal, 28 October 2015

The villagers of Bedlington   1183

Rare though it is, we do have some information about the life of ordinary village people near Morpeth not too long after the time of Juliana's marriage to Ranulph. Bedlington, just a few miles from Morpeth, was one of the bishop of Durham's outlying townships in south Northumberland. In 1183, the bishop Hugh de Puiset ordered a summary of all the obligations his townships owed him, and they are recorded in what is known as the *Boldon Book.*

In Bedlington, the men owed the following duties to their lord, in their case the bishop.

> One cart-load of wood and they mow the whole meadow (of the bishop) and lift and cart the hay and make ricks, and with the help of the other townships of Bedlingtonshire, they cart timber and mill-stones, and they similarly make the mill-pond, and they similarly enclose the court, and they similarly cover the hall, and they similarly prepare the fishery, and they similarly carry loads as far as Newcastle and as far as Fenwick and no further.[198]

We also learn the about agreements made by some of the men in replacement of other obligations.

> Turkill, who was the Bishop's man, renders 12 hens for his discharge from the Bishop. Cadewin pays 12 hens. Patrick renders 1 pound of pepper.[199]

> Robert son of Gospatrick pays 24 hens. Arnald son of Uchtred renders 12 hens. William Newton 6 hens. Ralph son of William 12 hens.[200]

There is one woman, Agnes Maddock, who is named in this section of the Boldon Book. Along with Robert of Choppington, she is exempt from certain services including the need to grind her corn in the bishop's mill.

> The Lord Bishop granted to Robert of Choppington and Agnes Maddock that they should be exempt ... from obligation to use the mill. And they hold 2 carucates of land with appurtenances in Choppington. And for this release they will give each year 25 shillings of which the aforesaid Robert will give 20 shillings. And Agnes 5 shillings.[201]

All this was happening close to Morpeth, and there is every reason to suppose that the ordinary people within the de Merlay barony lived similar lives. They would work for the baron, haymaking and carting, repairing his buildings, and paying renders with hens. Some might have negotiated money or other payments instead of work. How surprised they would have been, could they have known then, that we would be interested in their daily lives nine hundred years later.

Feeding the orphan babies

Coming from her family castle at Dunbar, Juliana would have been part of the tradition of noble ladies' families giving succour to the poor. She might well have followed the example of Queen Margaret of Scotland, to whom she was distantly related.

> The queen caused to be brought in to her in the first hour of the day nine baby orphans, destitute of all support: she had ordered the softer foods, in which the age of babyhood delights, to be prepared for them each day; and when they were brought she deigned to place them on her knees; to make their little drinks for them, and to put food into their mouths with the spoons that she used herself. Thus the queen who was honoured by the whole population filled for Christ's sake the part of a servant and the kindest mother.

There is more.

---

[198] John Morris and David Austin, Boldon Book, Phillimore, 1982, p 29
[199] As above, p 31
[200] As above, p 33
[201] As above, p 31

The custom was to bring in meanwhile, into the royal palace, three hundred poor. These were seated around in order; and when the king and queen had entered, the servants closed the doors: because, excepting certain religious chaplains and other attendants, none was permitted to be present at their works of charity. The king taking the one side, the queen taking the other, they served Christ in the poor; and with great devotion offered them food and drink specially prepared for the purpose.[202]

Queen Margaret's daughter Matilda, who had married King Henry I in 1100, took after her mother. One night, her brother David, later the king of Scotland, was summoned to his sister's presence.

He left the young courtiers with whom he was feasting and found her hall at Westminster full of lepers, and herself, suitably attired for the occasion, washing and drying and kissing their feet. She was a true daughter of Margaret, and he was a true son, but he none the less vigorously remonstrated, pointing out that Henry, should he come to hear of kisses such as these, might well be sparing of his own. Matilda informed her brother that she had summoned him in order that he might learn from her example, but he only laughed and withdrew.[203]

There is one trace of evidence of the charitable tradition during the time of the married life of Ranulph and Juliana. An infirmary for the poor was established in Morpeth, and William de Merlay, almost certainly their son in this instance, gave it some land for their support. Hodgson tells us this.

William de Merlay and his men, about the middle of the twelfth century, gave to the house of the infirm persons of Morpeth, for the souls of his father and mother, their ancestors, and himself, and for the forgiveness of their sins, one carucate of land, in free alms, and for ever. This is the only mention I have met with of this house. [204]

Did Juliana in her role as mistress of the castle on the hill feed orphan babies, invite the poor into her home, wash and kiss the feet of lepers, or encourage her son to support the infirmary? We don't know. We may suggest however that Juliana would have acted in the same spirit as Queen Margaret of Scotland and Queen Matilda of England here in Morpeth. I like to think that she did.

The fundamental date of 1129
Ranulph became the baron after the death of his father, William de Merlay, in 1129. Very soon after that, he ensured that his father's donation of Morwick to the monks of Durham was confirmed. This is the charter that gives us the fundamental date of 1129, bearing as it does the witness of William, the couple's oldest son.

Here is the charter. I have drawn attention to significant names in bold.

And after the death of William de Merlay, his son Ranulph, who was his heir, came to Durham in the year of our Lord 1129, in the month of September, the next day after the feast of saint Cuthbert, and gave, and conceded, and confirmed, and on the tomb of saint Cuthbert, with a small knife, offered this land, known as Morwick, to saint Cuthbert and the monks of Durham, freely and peacefully, from all misrepresentations, and free from all services, and from all customs for ever.

To this grant and confirmation all present as witnesses affirm.

The Prior of Tynemouth, Remigius
Robert the archdeacon
John of Mundaville
Wiiliam the son of Ranulph
Eustorcia the sister of Ranulph
Richard Tyson

---

[202] Turgot, Life of Queen Margaret, in Surtees Society Vol 51; also in Early Sources of Scottish History, p 78
[203] Ritchie, p 127
[204] Hodgson, Morpeth, p 76 and p 105

Robert the son of the Norman Bruce of Bointon
Ranulph Blaca
Eilaf priest of Hexham
Helias priest of Morpeth
William priest of Stannington
Gamel of Aclet
Melded of Aclet
Roger Conyers
Robert Firberne
Radulph of Wincester
Unfreth brother of Robert son of Norman
Edulf of Salwic
Paganus steward
Ranulph de Merle
Unspac Clibern
John of Widdrington
Ausk of Mundaville
Gancel son of Edred
Edmund son of Acult
Mervin of Hethworth[205]

Juliana and the younger children stayed at home, but Ranulph took his sister Eustorcia along. As far as I know, it is the only reference to him having a sister. There must have been discussions in the castle at Morpeth beforehand, and I can imagine Ranulph's younger sons, saying: "*Mon père*, it's not fair. Why can't I go too?"

It would have been an important and inspiring occasion. There were high level ecclesiastics among the witnesses, including the prior of Tynemouth and Robert the archdeacon. There was also a cluster of local priests including those from Hexham and Morpeth. And there is an interesting combination of English and Norman names, Eilaf, Unfreth and Edulf examples of the former, and Robert, Richard and John of the latter. In 1129, four decades after William de Merlay obtained Morpeth, the two nationalities seem to have settled in together.

This charter of 1129 takes us full circle to the beginning of this story. It was the year when young William signed the charter, and from that it was possible to estimate the date of the marriage of his parents.

---

[205] Hodgson, Morpeth, p 105; Dugdale, Monasticon Anglicanum, 1817 edn, p 241

Whispers around Ha' Hill

We are reaching the end of our story. The ancient earls of Northumberland had fought against the loss of their lands, but the Norman invaders had been stronger. Yet after the exile of her grandfather, the Earl Gospatric, the young bride returned to the homeland. When she married the future baron of Morpeth, she brought some of the lost lands with her as her dowry.

The couple successfully reared three boys. William, Roger and Osbert grew up and played around the castle on the hill, surely enjoying games in the river, learning to catch fish and ride horses, to hunt deer and small game, and to use bow and arrow, sword and shield.

As we wander through Morpeth's park nowadays along the river side, we can see the dome of Ha' Hill lying there solid and calm, grazed by sheep. In its shadow, children and teenagers practise their skills in the skateboard park, and people play tennis and mini-golf. There is no trace now of the timber castle that was Juliana's home; where her husband Ranulph welcomed her; where they talked and thought and argued; where they ate and entertained in their two languages; where they made love and brought forth a new generation.

In our journey together, we have learned the stories that Juliana would have told her children; about her rampaging grandfather; how her father negotiated with the king of England; and how she came to Morpeth. We know too that Ranulph would have told them about his father's adventures in the conquest of England, about Earl Robert de Mowbray and the capture of the castle at Morpeth. The motte by the river is still and silent now, but amid the cries of the youngsters on their scooters and skateboards if we pause for a moment we may hear their voices whispering in the breeze.

....

And then …

In the year 1138, Ranulph and Juliana donated some of the lands of her dowry to the monks of Newminster Abbey which they established near Morpeth.

Their son William grew up to become the baron, but he had no children as far as is known, and his brother Roger took his place at some date after 1162. Osbert was later described as *magister,* or teacher. He was buried with his parents in the abbey which they had founded, so perhaps he died young.

As for Juliana, daughter of Gospatric, the heirs of her body through her son Roger de Merlay survived for some more generations in Northumberland. That is a story for another time.

Appendix I   **The chroniclers and historians**

Tucked among the impressive works of the chroniclers and historians below is the information upon which the story of Juliana and Ranulph and early Morpeth is based. Some biographical details are taken from the *Oxford Dictionary of National Biography* and Wikipedia.

Simeon or Symeon of Durham   **writing 1090 – 1129**
Simeon was a monk and chronicler of Durham Priory in the late eleventh and early twelfth century. He, or others among his circle, wrote two well-known works which are frequently quoted in this history. The first is the *Libellus de Exordio Atque Procurso Istius hoc est Dunhelmensis Ecclesiae*, or *Tract on the Origin and Progress of the Church of Durham*. This is often shortened to *Libellus de Exordio* and translated as the *History of the Church of Durham*. The second is the *Historia Regum Anglorum et Dacorum* or the *History of the Kings of England*.

He wrote in the first three decades of the twelfth century. In *The History of the Kings* he took the section scanning the years 957 to 1119 largely from the chronicles of John or Florence of Worcester (see below), with some of his own insertions. The section from 1119 to 1129 is his own narrative and written with close knowledge of events which happened during his own lifetime.

Both these books include vivid descriptions of events found our story. I used the versions translated by Joseph Stevenson in 1855, part of the series called *The Church Historians of England*.

Orderic Vitalis   **living 1075 – c 1142**
Born in England, Orderic Vitalis was removed as a child to St Evroult monastery in Normandy where he completed his education and spent the rest of his life. His history moves with ease between England and Normandy, which at that time was almost a united kingdom, when many of its most prominent characters were active in both places.

He wrote *The Ecclesiastical History of England and Normandy* in Latin during the first decades of the twelfth century, covering the period 1050 to 1141. In translation it is an exceptionally useful and readable source of the history of Anglo-Norman world, and close to the timespan of the story of Juliana and Ranulph. He has stories about several of our characters, and is one of my most important sources.

I used the translation by Thomas Forester from 1853. There is a modern version by Marjorie Chibnall to which I also referred.

Geffrei Gaimar   **writing 1136 and 1137**
Gaimar was an Anglo-Norman poet and historian of unknown origin. He wrote one of the oldest surviving histories in the French of his day, contrasting with the monastic chroniclers in that it was designed to flatter the Norman nobility. His work *Lestorie des Engles*, or the *The History of the English*, was probably written in 1136 and 1137. It is generally considered by historians to be a conscientious narrative. Its importance to our story is his account of the rebellion of 1095 by Earl Robert de Mowbray, which includes the first documented reference to the castle at Morpeth that I have found.

John or Florence of Worcester   **writing 1095 - 1140**
John was a Benedictine monk and chronicler probably responsible for work formerly attributed to Florence of Worcester, writing 1095 to 1140. He makes a few references to events in our story which are different in interpretation from the other chronicles. His works cover events during the 11th century and up to 1140.

Roger of Hoveden or Howden   **died 1201 or 1202.**
Roger was a parson of Howden in the East Riding of Yorkshire, and clerk and diplomat to Henry II. Later he joined the service of Hugh du Puiset, Bishop of Durham. He wrote two chronicles, *Gesta Henrici II Benedicti Abbatis*, and the *Chronica*, from which the rare reference to the death of Gospatric I in our story is taken.

Wace   **writing up to 1174**
Wace was a Norman poet who was born in Jersey and brought up in mainland Normandy. His work *Roman de Rou* was commissioned by Henry II. Much of this was devoted to the conquest of England, and is an important source of the role of Bishop Geoffrey of Coutances on the night before the Battle of Hastings. His account may have used eyewitness testimonies. He wrote in a Jersey dialect of Norman French.

John Leland   **living c. 1503 - 1552**

Leland was a poet and antiquary born in London a few years before the accession of Henry VIII in 1509, and was educated in Cambridge, Oxford and Paris. He became Henry's keeper of libraries before 1530, and began looking into documents concerning the dissolution of the monasteries. As a result, he decided to travel over England and Wales, which he did for six years, recording his observations and compiling his findings. These are known as the Itineraries and the Collectanea.

His comments on Morpeth and Alnwick have been quoted by Rev John Hodgson, and often appear in later histories. For the purpose of our history, his main significance is his inclusion of William de Merlay as a servant of Bishop Geoffrey of Coutances in the *Collectanea*. Also very important is his noting of Wiliam de Merlay being once a lord of Warkworth which appears in one of his itineraries

William Dugdale   **1605 – 1686**

Dugdale was an English antiquary and herald at the time of the civil war between the parliamentarians and royalists (1642 – 1660). He became an MA of the university of Oxford in 1644, where he worked as a bureaucrat in the royalist capital. During his time at Oxford he began to collect material for his later publications. He collaborated with Roger Dodsworth on the *Monasticon Anglicanum*, a collection of manuscripts and charters from the dissolved monasteries. This was published in 1665, and includes a rare reference to the Bishop of Coutances acting as earl of Northumberland.

He had read Leland's works, and it is from his referenced account of the de Merlay family in his *Baronage of England* that the information about William de Merlay being a servant of the Bishop of Coutances was tracked down. The *Baronage*, produced between 1675 and 1676, is also a source of information about the de Mowbray and d'Albini familes.

Rev John Hodgson   **1779 - 1845**

Hodgson is the historian of Northumberland *par excellence*. His works were compiled between 1820 and 1840 on a parish by parish basis.

His histories are easily available in Northumberland's and Newcastle's libraries and archives. I used them constantly, although they take a good deal of application. His Part II, Volumes i, ii and iii, cover many of the parishes of Northumberland. His Part III contains many charters and documents to which he refers in his other works. His history of Morpeth was one section of Part II, Volume ii, published in 1832. It includes well referenced information about the de Merlays, including some ancient charters in English or Latin. This section has been published separately by Frank Graham as *A History of Morpeth* in 1973 and can be found in local libraries.

Parishes which he did not cover were later completed in the series known as the *Northumberland County Histories*. See the following two historians.

Rev William Greenwell   **1820 - 1918**

Greenwell was an eminent local archaeologist, librarian and historian, and wrote the comprehensive and well referenced account of the Gospatric family in the section on Edlingham parish in Volume VII of the *Northumberland County History*, published in 1904, and compiled by J Crawford Hodgson. This is the source for many details of the histories of Juliana's father and grandfather. J Crawford Hodgson should not be confused with Rev John Hodgson, which is very easily done.

Herbert H E Craster   **1897 - 1959**

Craster was an eminent scholar, born in Northumberland, and who became librarian at the Bodleian in Oxford. He wrote Volume VIII of the *Northumberland County History* about Tynemouth parish, published in 1907. His work is the source for the details of Earl Robert de Mowbray's association with the church and castle of Tynemouth.

Percy Hedley   **writing 1962 – 1968**

This historian and researcher from Simonburn in Northumberland compiled the fundamental work, *Northumberland Families Volumes I and II* for the Society of Antiquaries of Newcastle upon Tyne, which was published in 1968. Volume I contains essential information for the study of the de Merlays, the de Mowbrays and the Gospatrics. The family trees which he compiled, with such dates as are available, are a hugely important source for anyone studying their history.

William Kapelle   **writing in 1979**

His book, *The Norman Conquest of the North: The Region and its Transformation, 1000 to 1135*, is an essential background work. Published in 1979, it is not the easiest of reads, but it contains the story in greatest of detail about the period when Juliana and Ranulph's antecedents were battling over and ultimately establishing the future of Northumberland. For anyone interested in reading in depth some of the aspects I've touched on, it cannot be bettered.

Richard Lomas
His work, County of Conflict: Northumberland from Conquest to Civil War, published in 1996, is another essential modern book. Less hard to read than William Kapelle's, it is a thorough work covering the periods 925 to 1237 and later, and has chapters on different aspects of medieval life related specifically to our county.

John Beeler   writing in 1960s
His book, *Warfare in England 1066 – 1189,* is not the kind of book that I normally like to read for pleasure. But his chapter on Robert de Mowbray's rebellion of 1095 was the most useful I have read in that it sent me back to the relevant sections of the chronicles of Orderic Vitalis and Florence of Worcester, and even more importantly to Gaimar, the poet whose mention of Morpeth in 1095 is the best evidence we have of the timber castle on the hill being built by that time.

Writers about the lives of women
Few records about the everyday lives of women in the medieval period, especially from the humbler population, have survived. The following four writers have made special study of this subject. Much of their work is inevitably from the several centuries after Juliana, but nevertheless they are all well worth reading. I've used extracts from all of their works, particularly in the final chapter about the kind of life Juliana would have led in Morpeth.

Olive Tomkeieff   writing in 1960s
Her book, Life in Norman England, gives knowledgeable and sympathetic details about everyday life, particularly sensitive to the lives of women.

Henrietta Leyser   writing in 1995
Her book, Medieval Women, is a social history focussing on England in the period 450 – 1500. She has chapters on *1066 for Women, Sex, Marriage and Motherhood, Women at Work, Peasant Women* and *Female Monasticism,* much of the material being of a somewhat later date than the time of Juliana.

Lisa M Bitel   writing in 2002
Her book, *Women in Early Medieval Europe,* is a history written from the viewpoint of women. The writer is professor of history at the university of Southern California, and her book is a strong feminist contribution to women's studies, with a European and multi-cultural perspective.

Patricia Skinner and Elisabeth van Houts   writing in 2011
Their book, *Medieval Writings on Secular Women* is a collection of records from across Europe. It includes sections on *Birth and Infancy, Girls and Young Women, Married Women and Mothers, Widows, Older Women and Death.*

And a final word of praise

Elsa Hamilton   writing in 2010
Her book, *Mighty Subjects: The Dunbar Earls in Scotland, c 1072 – 1289*, is essential reading for anyone interested in the full story Gospatric, earl of Northumberland, exiled to Dunbar, and his descendants well beyond the period of my story. It is detailed and fully referenced, and I found it very helpful. The first three chapters thoroughly cover the story of the first and second Gospatrics. Her work has given me important insights into the background to Juliana's story.

Leland's list, names and places (grammatical endings left as in document) (first mention only included)	English spellings	Names in the story of the trial, Stevenson version	English Historical Documents
Gul: Rufus; Alvertonam	King William Rufus	King William the younger	King William the younger
Sivardus	Siward		
Rex Gul: Rufus; Gul: epifcopum; Dunelmen; Hoveden; Welton; Everwikfhir; comes Campaniae; comes Richemont	King William Rufus; William Bishop of Durham Howden; Welton; Yorkshire; Count Campania Count Richmond	Offedene; Welletune; Yorkshire; p 733	Howden; Wellton; Yorkshire; p 611
Odoni and Alano comitibus divisit		Odo of Kent; Alan of Brittanny and Richmond; p 733 (notes)	Count Odo; Count Alan; p 611
Radulphus Paganellus vicecomes Ebor:		Ralph Paganell, sheriff at York Also perhaps same as Reginald Paganell; p 732; p 746	Ralph Paynel; p 611
Rogerus Pictavensis	Roger of Poitou	Roger Putavensis; p 735	Earl Roger of Poitou; p 613; p 615
Urso de Abetot serviens Gul: Rufi regis	Servant of King William Rufus	Urso de Habetot; p 737	Urse of Abbetot; p 614
Magna suit lis; Ebor:	Great dispute York	Lanfranc; Roger Bigod; Hugh de Beaumont; bishop of Coutances; Thomas archbishop York; p 737 - 740	Lanfranc; Roger Bigot, Hugh de Beaumont, Geoffrey de Coutances; Thomas Archbishop of York, p 615 - 616
Radulphus Piperellus	Ralph Peverell of Nottingham	Ralph Piperell; p 743	Ralph Peverel; p 619
Gul: de Merleio fervus epifcopi Conftantienfis	Servant of the bishop of Coutances	William de Merlay; p 746 Robert de Countville; p 747	William 'de Merlao'
Gualterus de Agencourt			
Ivo Taillebofc & Erneifus de Burone diffaifarverunt Gul: epifcopum de eccl: & de caftello Dunelmi, & de omni terra sua	Servants of William Bishop of church and castle of Durham	Ivo Taillesbosc; Ernes de Burone; p 747	Ivo Taillebosc, Ernesius 'de Burone'; p 622
Robertus de comitis villa		Roger de Mowbray; p 748 (This is Robert de Mowbray probably. Some confusions between names Robert and Roger de Mowbray here, noted by several historians.)	Roger of Mowbray; p 622
Robertus de infula Vectae		Robert de Insula, Richard de Cultura, Osmund bishop of Salisbury; p 748	
Hugo de Portu		Hugh de Port; p 749	
Gaufridus de Tracleio		Geoffrey de Trailly; p 749	

Appendix 3   Juliana's marriage charters

Carta Regia. Licence by king Henry I. to Ranulph de Merlay to marry Juliana, daughter of Earl Cospatric.

Henricus Rex Angl' et dux Norman' . . . ministris (et) omnibus Baronibus suis Francis et Anglicis (Northumbriæ), salutem. Notum sit omnibus vobis, me dedisse Ranulpho de Merlay Julianam filiam comitis Cospatricii, et sciatis quod inter me et patrem suum dedimus ei in liberum mariale, (sibi) atque hæredibus suis, scil. Horsley, Stanton, W(itton), Ritton', Wyndgates, et quandam villam ultra moras, ta(m liber)e quam aliquis potest liberius inter maria vel (alio) alicui dare tenendum in suo dominico. Et ex hoc præcipio (meis) Justiciariis ut videant quod nichil ei desit, et si aliquis ei contradicere voluerit, tunc præcipio Justiciariis et Vicecomitibus meis de Northumbria, ut plenum rectum ei teneant. Testibus, Patricio fil., Joha. Peuerell de Baelcamp', Willelmo de Allunbrito, Henr. fil. Johannis, Willelmo del Pont del Harche, Willelmo Maltrauar', Willelmo Maldut, apud Wodstok. Et Edgarus fil. Cospatri comitis confirmavit hanc cartam, ut sequitur in hæc verba.

Alia carta. Confirmation by Edgar, son of Earl Cospatric, of the dowry of his sister Juliana.

Edgarus Gospatri (*sic*) comitis filius, omn. amicis suis Francis et Anglis, salutem. Sciatis me dedisse concessisse Julianæ sorori meæ terram quam meus pater et suus, scil. Comes Gospatricus, ei dedit in franco mariagio et concessit, scil. Witton', Horsley, Stanton', Ritton', Wyndgates, et Leuerchilde, sibi et suis hæredibus hæredibus ex me et meis hæredibus in terris, in aquis, in forestis omnibus illis terris pertinentibus, et in silvis, in molendinis, in stagnis, in pratis, in pascuis, in viis et extra vias, et in rebus omnibus illis terris pertinentibus, exceptis tribus serviciis, videlicet comunis excersitus in Com', et cornagio, et comune opus castelli in Com'. Et volo ut tam libere et quiete teneat, ut meus pater ei dedit, has supradictas terras, in franco mariagio. Valete. Testante Johanne decano de Bewyk, Willelmo presbitero de Stanton', Ostredo presbitero de Hertborne, Alano clerico, Grimbauldo de Merlay, Willelmo fil. Elef, Sewert fil. Liolf et fil. ejus, Liolf fil. Liolf et Roberto fratre ejus, Cospatrico fil. Leuenoc, Cospatrico de Horsley et Alexandro fil. ejus, Chilinchet fratre ejus, et Willelmo fratre ejus, Alexandro fil. Hamunis (?), Aschetil de Stan(ton), Godfrid de Windegates, et multis aliis.

From the "ancient roll" appended to the Newminster Cartulary, transcribed by Rev J Fower, Surtees Society Volume 66, 1876, pp 268-269

Appendix 4   **The "spurious" charter**

Spurious – not genuine, not being what it purports to be. OED

There are two versions of Juliana's marriage charter in existence, wrote Rev William Greenwell in his 1904 article about the Gospatrics in the Northumberland County History, Vol VII, page 37. One is the version in the "ancient roll" appended to the Newminster Cartulary, which is copied in Appendix 3 here. The other, he wrote, "is in Scarborough Museum".

> It is without doubt spurious, and possibly is not of an earlier date than the sixteenth century. It is probably based upon a genuine charter, but with what object it was fabricated is not apparent. It is incorrectly printed from the original in the *Priory of Hexham,* vol. i. *Illustrative Documents,* p ix. The vellum is stained and otherwise damaged, and it is impossible to decipher some of the words.

He does however then follow with an attempt at transcribing it, in Latin, with all its faults.

Another place to find information about the "spurious" charter is the *Regesta Regum Anglo-Normannorum*, a calendar of documents from between 1066 and 1154. There are two charters summarised, both apparently signed at Woodstock between 1123 and 1132. The first is a summary of the version appended to the Newminster cartulary. The second however is the "spurious" one, summarised as follows.

> Notification by Henry I (King of England and Duke of Normandy) generally addressed to Northumberland: that he has given to Ralph de M[erlai] Julia[na] daughter of Earl Gospatric [with the manors assigned to her by her father] with the usual liberties [sac, soc etc] and the right to hunt hart, hind and boar.

The editors of this calendar of documents also call it a "mutilated, pseudo-original probably of the 16th century". Furthermore, on page xxi, they say this.

> The grants of sporting rights were usually limited by a reservation to the King of all "harts, hinds and swine" … and … the grant to Ralph de Merlai to hunt hart, hind and boar might safely be condemned on that account alone.

Because this "spurious" charter is unreliable, it is described here, rather than commented upon in the main text of this book.

Bibliography

Anderson, Alan Orr, translator, Early Sources of Scottish History, Paul Watkins, Stamford, 1990

Anglo Saxon Chronicles, Anne Savage, Bramley, 1997; also English Historical Documents, see Douglas

Barrow, G W S, The Anglo-Norman Era in Scottish History, Clarendon, 1980

Beeler, John, Warfare in England, Cornell University, 1966

Bitel, Lisa, Women in Early Medieval Europe, Cambridge, 2002

Blair, C H Hunter, The Early Castles of Northumberland; Archaeologica Aeliana, 4th Series, 1944; and Baronys and Knights of Northumberland, Archaeologia Aeliana, 4th Series, 1952

Blair, Peter Hunter, Some Observations on the Historia Regum, in Celt and Saxon, ed Nora Chadwick, Cambridge, 1963

Boldon Book, see Morris below

Book of Fees, HMSO, 1923

Bristow, Joy, The Local Historian's Glossary of Words and Terms, Countryside Books, 2001

Calendar of Documents relating to Scotland, Joseph Bain, Edinburgh

Craster, H H E, Northumberland County History, Vol VIII and
        The Red Book of Durham, English Historical Review, 1925 at SANT library, I 48/24

Crosby, Everett, The King's Bishops, Palgrave, 2013

Dictionnaire de la Noblesse, de la Chenaye-Desbois et Badier, Editions 1775 and 1868

Dictionnaire du pays d'Argentan, Le Merlerault, 1965

Douglas, David and Greenaway, George, English Historical Documents 1042 – 1189, Eyre and Spottiswoode,1953

Dugdale, Sir William, Baronage of England, 1675-76, Vol 2; this edition printed 1675

Dugdale, John, Monasticon Anglicanum, Vol I, 1665; this edition by Cale, Ellis and Bandinel 1846

Early Sources of Scottish History, see Anderson above

English Historical Documents, see Douglas above

Florence of Worcester, (his works now believed to be by John of Worcester), translated by Thomas Forester, Bohn, London 1854

Gaimar, L'estoire des Engleis, 1136 – 1137, Eds Hardy and Martin, London HMSO, 1889

Greenwell, Rev William, The House of Gospatric, Northumberland County History, ed J C Hodgson, Vol VII, 1904

Gubbins, Bridget, Monks, Shepherds and Charters, GMDT, 2014

Hamilton, Elsa, Mighty Subjects, John Donald, 2010

Hedley, Percy W, Northumberland Families, Vol 1, 1968, Society of Antiquaries of Newcastle upon Tyne

Higham, N J, The Kingdom of Northumbria, AD 350 – 1100, Alan Sutton, 1993

Higham, Robert and Barker, Philip, Timber Castles, Batsford, 1992; and Hen Domen, Montgomery: a timber castle on the English-Welsh border, Exeter University Press, 2000

Historic Environment Record for Northumberland, 11068/8

Hodgson, John Crawford, ed, Northumberland County History, Vol VII, 1904

Hodgson, Rev John, History of Morpeth, 1832, Frank Graham reprint 1977

Hunter Blair, C, Archaeologia Aeliana Vol XX 4th series, 1944

Kapelle, William, The Norman Conquest of the North, London, 1979

Leland, John. Collectanea, Volume II, London, 1774

Leyser, Henrietta, Medieval Women, Phoenix, 1996

Liber Niger Scaccarii, ed T Hearne, 1771

Lomas, Richard, County of Conflict; Northumberland from Conquest to Civil War, Tuckwell, 1996

Mackenzie, E, A Historical and Descriptive View of the County of Northumberland, Vol 1,1811

Meehan, Bernard, Symeon of Durham, ODNB, 2004 - 2015

Miller, James, The History of Dunbar, 1859 (reprint, no publisher named)

Newminster Cartulary, Surtees Society Vol 66, 1878

Morris, John and Austin, David Austin, Boldon Book, Phillimore, 1982

O'Brien, Colm, Early Medieval Shires, Archaeologia Aeliana Vol XXX 5th series, 2002

Orderic Vitalis, Ecclesiastical History of England and Normandy, Thomas Forester, London, 1854

Patourel, John le, Geoffrey of Montbray, Bishop of Coutance, English Historical Review, 1944

Percy Cartulary, Surtees Society Vol 117, 1909 - 1911

Regesta Regum Anglo-Normannorum, 1066 – 1154, Vol 2, Johnson, Crone, Oxford Clarendon, 1956

Richard Prior of Hexham, Seeley, 1856

Ritchie, Graeme R L, The Normans in Scotland, Edinburgh, 1954

Roberts, Brian, Northumberland: reflections on prehistoric, Roman and Old English settlement, Archaeologia Aeliana, 5th series, Vol 44, 2015

Short, Ian, Oxford Dictionary of National Biography, 2004-15

Simeon, History of the Church of Durham, translated by Joseph Stevenson, 1855, republished by Llanerch, 1993

Simeon, History of the Kings of England, translated by Joseph Stevenson, 1858, republished by Llanerch, 1987

Skinner, Patricia and van Houts, Elisabeth, Medieval Writings on Secular Women, Penguin, 2011

Tomkeieff, Olive, Life in Norman England, Batsford, 1966

Toulmin Smith, Lucy, The Itinerary of John Leland 1535-1543, George Bell, London, 1907

Wace, The Conquest of England, translated Alexander Malet, London, Bell and Daldry 1860

Williams and Martin, Domesday Book, A Complete Translation, Penguin, 1992